Anonymus

Special Reports of Irish Land Commission on Discharge of Duties under 29th Section of Land Law (Ireland) Act, 1887

Anonymus

Special Reports of Irish Land Commission on Discharge of Duties under 29th Section of Land Law (Ireland) Act, 1887

ISBN/EAN: 9783742811165

Manufactured in Europe, USA, Canada, Australia, Japa

Cover: Foto ©Suzi / pixelio.de

Manufactured and distributed by brebook publishing software (www.brebook.com)

Anonymus

Special Reports of Irish Land Commission on Discharge of Duties

under 29th Section of Land Law (Ireland) Act, 1887

Trade Union Immunities

*Presented to Parliament by the Secretary of State for Employment
by Command of Her Majesty
January 1981*

LONDON
HER MAJESTY'S STATIONERY OFFICE
£5·30 net

Cmnd. 8128

CHAPTER 1

INTRODUCTION

1. A nation's prosperity rests ultimately on the ability of its people to live and work in harmony with each other. If its industrial relations are marked by conflict rather than cooperation the nation as a whole pays the price of economic stagnation. For at least a generation now our industrial relations have failed us because they have inhibited improvements in productivity, acted as a disincentive to investment and discouraged innovation. The results are apparent in our poor industrial performance and lower standard of living compared with our major competitors overseas.

2. The incidence of strikes and other forms of industrial action in this country is the most evident manifestation of the inadequacy of our industrial relations, but it is by no means the only one. The persistence of restrictive practices, of outdated working methods and of overmanning have contributed just as powerfully, if more insidiously, to our economic problems. Such practices and the attitudes they embody have stood in the way of the achievement of high productivity, high output and high real wages.

3. The freedom of employees to combine and to withdraw their labour is their ultimate safeguard against the inherent imbalance of power between the employer and the individual employee. This freedom has come to be accepted as a hallmark of a free society. But implicit in that acceptance is the assumption that this freedom will be used responsibly, that industrial action will be taken only with proper regard for the interests of others and of the community as a whole. In times of national emergency, for example, greater restraint is expected—and has been shown—in the use of this essentially disruptive power.

4. The importance of the freedom to combine to withdraw labour in the face of serious grievances at work is not in question. What is questioned is the readiness to threaten and deploy the strike weapon with apparent disregard for the consequences, whether for the future of the enterprises affected, for the jobs and livelihoods of their employees or for the rest of the community. Many strikes effectively repudiate agreements made by those organising them or by their representatives and the vast majority are called without reference to senior trade union officials and without their endorsement. All too often the strike or the threat of a strike is a tactic of first instead of last resort. And, when strikes occur, the degree of disruption is sometimes quite disproportionate to the grievance felt. Industrial action is extended deliberately to harm employees who have no interest in the dispute and pushed even further to inflict the maximum hardship and inconvenience on the community. Moreover, the mere threat of a strike can in some circumstances be as effective a weapon as a strike itself. The readiness to threaten industrial action has imposed serious obstacles to necessary change, greater efficiency and improved performance in many of our industries. As a result our ability to compete in home and overseas markets has seriously declined.

5. All this has led to questioning of the scope which the law permits to industrial action and to a wider debate about the role of trade unions and management in our society. These have long been a matter of controversy. For at least a hundred years there has been argument about the acceptable balance of bargaining power between employees and their employers and the duties they and their representatives owe to the nation. Industrial relations cannot operate fairly and efficiently or to the benefit of the nation as a whole if either employers or employees collectively are given predominant power—that is, the capacity effectively to dictate the behaviour of others. What the law can achieve in affecting the balance of power must not be over-estimated, but it has always been recognised as a proper role of Parliament to intervene by statute to correct manifestations—whether by employers or employees—of a disequilibrium of bargaining power.

6. A rational and informed public debate about the law and practice of industrial relations is now essential. Such a debate took place in the years following the Donovan Commission[1] report. It must now be resumed. Many of the problems identified then have remained or intensified. Our success as a manufacturing and trading nation depends crucially on the improvement of our industrial relations.

7. It is not possible for the debate to be joined without an understanding of the long and often turbulent history of our industrial relations and the way in which the present legal framework has developed. Nor is it possible to ignore the deep emotions which have been aroused in that process and which are still evident. Britain was the first country to face the problems of accommodating the phenomenon of trade unions within its legal system. Against the background of an uncodified system of law and an unwritten Constitution, the approach adopted was to exempt trade unions from the prohibition of conduct "in restraint of trade" to which many of their activities would otherwise have been liable and to provide them with immunities from legal actions under both the criminal and civil law. The law today still takes this form.

8. Other countries with different legal traditions and constitutional frameworks have taken a different approach. They have elected instead to give trade unions positive but defined rights. In Britain there is no specific legal right to strike. An employee who takes industrial action in breach of his contract of employment faces the risk of lawful dismissal or other sanctions. But since the 1870s, the law has provided immunity against charges of criminal conspiracy for those who organise industrial action and, since 1906, immunities for individuals and trade unions against being sued in tort.[2] In

[1] "Royal Commission on Trade Unions and Employers' Associations (1965–8)"; Chairman: Lord Donovan (June 1968, Cmnd 3623, HMSO).

[2] There are two systems of law in Great Britain—one covering England and Wales, the other, Scotland. While they differ, particularly in terminology, they are very similar in effect in the field of immunities from civil actions with which this Green Paper is concerned. The text of this Green Paper does not therefore distinguish between the two systems and for the sake of brevity it uses the terminology of the English system. In particular the English legal terms "tort" and "injunction" are used to cover their Scottish equivalents of "delict" and "interdict".

this way the law gives British trade unions a position for which there is no parallel in other countries. These immunities mean that, in certain circumstances, employers who would otherwise have been able to bring civil proceedings to secure redress against those organising industrial action are prevented from doing so. These immunities protect trade unions against having their officials imprisoned or penalised in the courts for organising trade union activities, and their funds drained away in civil proceedings.

9. This method of giving legality to collective industrial action through immunities has been criticised on two general grounds. First, it is argued that it leaves the boundaries of lawful industrial action unclear and consequently more subject to determination in the courts than is desirable. One result of this is that the "rights" of trade unions and their officials have been asserted without the development of corresponding obligations or protection for the individual worker against trade union power. Secondly, it has satisfied neither employers nor trade unions: many employers, particularly if they are not parties to a dispute, are reluctant to accept that they should be deprived of what they see as their normal rights in law to seek redress against damage to their business, while it has made trade unionists defensive and suspicious in their attitude to both the legislature and the courts, particularly when the courts have had to deal with cases on the borderline of immunity. One of the issues considered in this Green Paper (Chapter 4) is the extent to which a "positive" legal right to take collective industrial action—such as exists in other countries—might avoid or temper these criticisms.

10. In examining this and other options it must be remembered that the way in which the law on industrial action has developed so far in this country has been characteristic of our industrial relations as a whole. Compared with most other countries there has traditionally been a minimum of legal interference and regulation. The conduct of our industrial relations is basically voluntary. It is dependent primarily on managements and trade unions sorting out problems and differences for themselves and developing their own agreed procedures, arrangements and practices, as well as the institutions which embody them. We have no great tradition of legally enforceable agreements as there is, for example, in Sweden—although there has been nothing to prevent managements and unions concluding them if they wished. There is no tradition of compulsory arbitration as there is in Australia; no tradition of resorting to the courts or to legally binding arbitration to resolve disputes which arise from collective agreements as there is in the USA.

11. The Donovan Commission in 1968 described the British system of industrial relations as:

"based on voluntarily agreed rules which, as a matter of principle, are not enforced by law. This is an outstanding characteristic which distinguishes it from the systems of many comparable countries. No trade union, no employer in private industry, no employers' association, is under any legal obligation to bargain collectively; and, exceptions apart, the law does not intervene to enforce such a bargain, or any of its terms. The law has done little to restrict or otherwise to

regulate the use of industrial sanctions such as the strike and the lock out. A right to strike has never been formulated in positive terms, but statutes have been enacted to remove obstacles which the common law placed in the way of the use of industrial sanctions. With very few exceptions, the law prevents no one from joining a trade union, and protects no one against attempts made by others to impede the exercise of his freedom of association. The law has never been called upon to help in organising or operating a system of workers' representation at enterprise or at plant level . . . . In short, it has been the traditional policy of the law as far as possible not to intervene in the system of industrial relations''.
(paragraph 751)

The avoidance of legal intervention in collective bargaining appears to have been pursued as a matter of principle by both employers and trade unions alike. It is clear, for example, that as long ago as the legislation of 1906 trade unions preferred to proceed by way of immunities, rather than accept liability as corporate bodies with consequent legal responsibilities.

12. However, over the last twenty years the role of the law in industrial relations has been considerably extended. This extension has, in the main, taken the form of new statutory rights for the individual employee and corresponding obligations for his employer. The effect of this has been to create a dual framework of law in industrial relations. The role of the law remains non-interventionist as it affects trade unions, but it has clearly become more interventionist as it affects employers. No obligations have been placed on the unions to use new procedures established by law or to adopt them as alternatives to industrial action, but many additional obligations have been placed on employers. Partly as a result of this, there has developed a widespread public feeling, not least among trade union members, that trade unions have too few obligations and too much power. This has been coupled with a growing concern over the impact on the community of unregulated industrial action. It has brought into focus the issue of the role of the law in restraining excesses and abuses of industrial power and it has led to renewed questioning of the legal framework within which employers and unions operate.

13. What is the role of the law in improving industrial relations? Where a society has a tradition of legal regulation in industrial relations—as in West Germany—the law has a better chance, over the years, of reinforcing and encouraging responsible behaviour on both sides. But in Britain, where there is a different tradition, attempts to secure reform by means of legal restraint on trade union power have had to contend with obstructive and uncooperative attitudes. If the law is to be respected and to play a useful role in changing behaviour these attitudes have to be overcome. The law by itself cannot change such attitudes overnight. The Industrial Relations Act 1971 was frustrated both because trade unions were able to build a concerted campaign of opposition to it and because employers did not generally see it as in their immediate interests to make use of its provisions. The contribution which changes in the law can make must be seen in the context of our still predominantly voluntary system and of the far reaching

4

changes in the nature of trade union power, of industrial action and of the labour market over the last two decades and more. In particular, proposals for changing the law which are designed to influence the behaviour of trade unions as formally organised institutions, but which ignore the reality of shop floor power and the current propensity for unofficial action, are unlikely to be effective at either level.

14. The uncertain legal status of trade unions in their formative years has inevitably influenced their attitudes to the law. Trade unions came into existence in the nineteenth century despite the law and not under its protection. They developed voluntarily as workers came together to use their collective strength to offset the power of the employer to hire and fire and to provide for their members in times of need. That collective power has its expression in the threat of withdrawal of labour. Without it trade unions in Britain would have no effective sanction against employers. It is ultimately that power—not any legally enforceable right to be informed, consulted or involved in decision making—which trade union leaders bring to the negotiating table. It is a power which, in the end, stems from the shopfloor, from the members.

15. A shift of power has been taking place in the trade union movement; from the centre to the shopfloor, from full-time officials of the unions to shop stewards drawn from those among whom they work. It is reflected in the tendency for plenary power to call industrial action, negotiate and settle to be seized by the shopfloor or delegated to it. In other countries, such as the USA, Sweden and West Germany, union leaders at national level have substantive authority. This is apparent, for example, in their capacity to negotiate effective long-term, legally binding, collective agreements. But, in Britain, it is the more active union members—and their lay shopfloor leaders—who have increasingly taken the lead in collective bargaining. The development of this informal system of management/trade union relationships alongside the formal system was clearly indentified by the Donovan Commission. Its effect in the years since 1968 has been to weaken the authority of many large trade unions and to make the task of their leaders and of the TUC more difficult. It has been associated with an increase in unofficial industrial action to the extent that some 90 per cent of strikes are now unofficial. It has been accentuated by the impact of technological change and the increased interdependence of firms and industries, giving to small groups on the shopfloor—such as computer operators—enormous disruptive power.

16. The Donovan Commission saw the solution to these problems in the integration of the formal system of industrial relations with the informal. The last decade has seen some increase in structured plant bargaining but the benefits the Donovan Commission envisaged flowing from this in terms of improved procedures and a reduction in industrial conflict have not been achieved. The problems remain. Even within the "formal" system, a single employer in Britain may still have to negotiate with as many as twenty different unions, often with competing and incompatible objectives, and he may be unable to establish common bargaining arrangements for employees whose work is closely linked. The process of trade union

5

amalgamation has been relatively slow and piecemeal and not always directed towards securing improved collective bargaining arrangements. Those changes in trade union structure which have taken place have occurred in response to organic developments in industry, such as the growth of white collar and public service unions, or to alterations in the balance between groups within particular trade unions, such as the development of shop stewards' combines as a result of the growth of plant bargaining. But these changes in individual trade unions have not always been reflected in the structure of the TUC and sometimes they have created direct conflict between local and national leaders. It can be argued that unless the trade union movement comes to more rational structures for the conduct of collective bargaining, it cannot best serve the interests of its members or contribute to improved economic performance and the benefits this would provide to the community as a whole.

17. Whilst the old problems of our industrial relations remain and indeed have been intensified by developments in the years since the Donovan Commission, new pressures from outside have put a more urgent emphasis still on the search for solutions. Industry and jobs are changing at an ever faster rate under the impact of increasingly sophisticated technology. New jobs are arising in the service sector rather than in manufacturing and in white collar rather than blue collar occupations; and there is a growing need for new skills and for a greater readiness to acquire them, to change jobs and to retrain in the course of a working life. These developments confront new generations whose attitudes are themselves evolving. Our workforce is now generally better educated than before, more highly unionised and less deferential, both to management and trade union leaders.

18. These developments have put a great strain on our industrial relations. There is a pressing need for both trade unions and management to develop a capacity to respond to change. But this is frustrated because our industrial relations are shackled by suspicion and deeply resistant to change.

19. It is against this perspective that the role of the law has to be assessed. Changes in the law can influence attitudes and behaviour over time. The Employment Act 1980 provided new protection against the identified, worst abuses. But good industrial relations cannot simply be legislated into existence. Reform must also come from within: from trade unions and employers adapting their institutions and practices to the social and economic pressures for change.

20. For the trade unions an essential element in this process must be to ensure that they are fully representative of their members and responsive to their wishes and interests. It is still rare for unions to consult their members directly on major decisions which affect them deeply. In only a few unions is the leadership elected by postal ballot of all the members. In some cases, once elected, national officials are not required to submit themselves for re-election. The internal authority of trade unions over their members will always be inadequate if their leaders are felt to be out of touch with those they represent and without proper democratic procedures

there will inevitably be suspicions that trade unions sometimes pursue policies which the majority of their members do not support. If trade unions are to restore their authority and regain or sustain the confidence of their members they must be fully democratic both in the way they take critical decisions and in the method of electing their officials. This means, for example, making greater use of postal ballots to consult the membership on such questions as the calling of industrial action (see Chapter 3 Section F) and to elect (and re-elect) their leaders. Trade unions can no longer reasonably claim that they are inhibited from holding postal ballots by virtue of expense. Under the Employment Act public funds are now available for postal ballots for union elections and votes on other important issues.

21. Employers share the responsibility for the present state of our industrial relations. Many of the inadequacies of our present system and the barriers to greater productivity and efficiency are the result of employer attitudes and practices which, in their way, are just as inflexible and outdated as the trade union practices described in earlier paragraphs. The tendency of employers, particularly in times of full employment, to look for the short-term solutions in relations with their employees and trade union officials without regard to the long-term consequences has stored up a legacy of inefficiency and restrictive practices from which we are now suffering.

22. Employers have over the years paid too little attention to their industrial relations policies. They have been reluctant in their collective bargaining arrangements to enter into precise or legal commitments as much as have trade unions. They have been disinclined to seek legally enforceable agreements, preferring in general imprecise arrangements, so unclear and ambiguous in some cases that to have translated them into legally binding agreements would have been very difficult.

23. Employers have also contributed to the growth in authority of shop-floor representatives. The easy accessibility of shop stewards and local lay officers compared with the frequently overworked, full-time officials has proved attractive to management seeking a rapid solution to "wildcat" action; they have often been ready to enter into negotiations with "unofficial" elements to the detriment of the authority of more senior officials.

24. Above all, employers have shown too little willingness to involve employees and their representatives in policies and decisions which affect their working lives. As a result employees, particularly in large companies, feel remote from the centre of decision making in their firm and powerless to influence the running of their enterprise. In turn this makes them distrustful of changes in their working practices and of the introduction of new techniques. The failure of many managements to adopt coherent and consistent policies to involve and communicate with employees, or to show sufficient sensitivity towards the legitimate hopes and fears of their workforce, continues to make the task of responsible trade union leaders more difficult and nourishes the distrust and defensiveness occasioned by former failures.

25. The responsibility for initiating changes in this area clearly rests with managers. It is not simply a matter of developing new machinery for involving employees or increasing the flow of information about the company but a readiness to extend the range of matters on which they are prepared to consult and to take their employees into their confidence. Unions in their turn must be ready to meet managements half way and respond positively to their initiatives.

26. If consultation comes too late—only when there is bad news or an unpopular decision to impart—the results will inevitably be negative and discouraging. The essence of employee involvement lies in involving employees at the points at which they wish to be involved and where they have a specific and direct interest in being involved. To be successful it must fit the individual circumstances and the perceived needs of both employer and employees. It is therefore best developed voluntarily and not imposed by legislation. It must be seen to be effective and relevant. It must not be limited to minor issues and not seen as a substitute for collective bargaining to be pursued with some unrealistic idea of removing all conflict of interest in industry. If our industrial relations are to improve, managements and unions in industry must genuinely desire cooperation and must work to achieve it. That is the key in a modern industrial society to higher productivity, real competitiveness, greater profits and greater rewards for employees.

27. It is within the enterprise that a real improvement is most necessary. We need effective management prepared to be firm and to give a lead, but which is understanding and sensitive to the views, interests and aspirations of their employees. We need trade unions who are able to defend their members' interests robustly but who recognise that job security and increased rewards can only come from an efficient industry competing in world markets.

28. But there are also issues of a wider and more fundamental importance for the future of our society which need to be tackled if workable solutions to the detailed problems discussed in this Green Paper are to be found. As the Donovan Commission pointed out, the role of law has to be seen as one factor only in an evolutionary process which is conditioned also by institutions, conventions and understandings. Indeed, all discussion of the law must inevitably involve judgements—both implicit and explicit—about the wider context: in particular, about the duties which trade unions and employers owe to the community as a whole. Are they merely pressure groups with obligations only to their own members and no duty to take a wider view? Or have they already, by virtue of a very long if informal relationship with the state and their importance in the running of a complex modern economy, become bodies of a different type whose influence and concomitant duties have, however, not yet been properly defined?

29. The continuing absence of a well-defined, stable and publicly accepted relationship between trade unions, employers' organisations and the Government has contributed to damaging dissension both in industrial relations and more widely. Both trade unions and employers' associations

have had more or less continuing right of access to Ministers and departments of state. Unions and employers have also had a balanced representation on Royal Commissions and other Committees of Inquiry. The National Economic Development Council (NEDC) has been established and maintained as a permanent forum in which both groups can voice their concerns on issues of the day.

30. The effectiveness of this practice, however, as an aid to the good government of the nation has been limited. It has not led to a meeting of minds on important issues. Rather, it has led to fresh arguments with a strong emotional content about what sort of relationship is "necessary" or "legitimate" for these purposes. There has been little evidence that the involvement of the leaders of employers' and trade union organisations in national affairs has led to greater understanding of the issues amongst their members, whether in the boardroom or at shopfloor level. Here again, we have failed where other nations have succeeded in establishing stable working relationships which both recognise the need for change and smooth its path. At no time have we in Britain needed to rebuild from scratch work people's and employers' organisations as had to be done in Germany in the late 1940s.

31. The sensible running of industry and the wider interests of the community have frequently been frustrated by the incapacity of either trade unions or employer organisations to enter into agreements or undertakings commensurate with the influence they have claimed to possess. These problems cannot be resolved simply or quickly. It can be argued that for that reason they should not be discussed at all; that they confuse issues which can better be dealt with in a pragmatic way; or that they create political friction which should be avoided. On the other hand, it is argued that there is now an opportunity to clarify the essential differences which distinguish the functions, duties and rights of these bodies from those of political parties, Parliament and the Government and to set out what the relationship between each of them should be.

32. The absence of reasoned debate leading to a wider understanding of common problems seriously hampers progress. If it were possible to establish clear and acceptable relationships between these dissimilar bodies as a working understanding, the incessant flexing of industrial muscle to impress Government might be replaced by more constructive activity. The realisation of such a working understanding, freely entered into for mutual advantage and for the greater good of the community, would require a high degree of responsibility and education. It is an area where Government could be of tangible help, though not one where it could—or should—seek to impose solutions. Questions of the day already find a focus in the NEDC. This practice could be expanded with advantage.

33. The purpose of this Green Paper is to prompt a wide and informed debate on the law concerning industrial action and on the role in modern life of trade unions and employers and their duties and obligations. The recognition of the crucial need to make progress in building a better climate

9

for improvements in industrial relations will help to produce a fuller and more considered debate on all the issues involved than has taken place for many years. This paper is designed to provide information and ideas which can stimulate that debate. Chapter 2 describes how the present law on immunities has developed since the nineteenth century. Chapter 3 discusses a wide range of proposals which have been put forward for amending the existing system of immunities. Chapter 4 examines the case for and the feasibility of moving to a new legal framework based on "positive rights". But discussion of the law naturally involves consideration of the wider questions raised in the concluding paragraphs of this introductory Chapter, about relations between trade unions and employer organisations and between both these groups and Government.

CHAPTER 2

THE HISTORY AND DEVELOPMENT OF TRADE UNION IMMUNITIES

34. In those countries in which strikes and other forms of industrial action are legally recognised the law is generally couched in the form of a positive right to strike subject to various restraining conditions and qualifications, as described later in Chapter 4. In Great Britain, for historical reasons, the law has taken a quite different form. The law governing strikes and other industrial action is based on a series of legal immunities which protect those who organise and take part in trade disputes from both criminal and civil liability. Without these immunities most industrial action would be illegal. Trade unions, their officials and their members would be liable to criminal prosecution or to civil actions for damages every time they were involved in a strike unless due notice to terminate contracts of employment were given.

35. To understand what legal immunities are, and how they have developed, it is necessary to trace their development from the nineteenth century. This Chapter does not attempt to provide a comprehensive history of trade unions and industrial law. It concentrates on the history and development of the law as it relates to industrial action.

Industrial action and the common law

36. The starting point for consideration of immunities is the common law itself. The common law provides the basic legal precepts and principles which underlie all subsequent law. It can be abrogated and modified by Acts of Parliament but, subject to this, it is according to their interpretation of the common law that the courts decide cases which are brought before them.

37. The history of trade union law since the middle of the nineteenth century, when trade unions were developing, has in general been one of a step by step development of statutory protections against common law liabilities: first, in the nineteenth century, against criminal liabilities such as criminal conspiracy; then, in the twentieth century, against civil liabilities for tort. The process has been one of interaction between legislation and the common law. This is because the common law itself has always been developing, sometimes in ways seen by trade unions to be in conflict with the developing scope of their own activities.

38. Britain is not, of course, unique in having to define the status of trade unions and industrial action in law. What is unique is the way in which it has been done: not, as in other countries, through positive rights, but rather through a system of legal immunities.

Immunities in the nineteenth century

39. For most of the nineteenth century trade union organisation and activity was most at risk from the criminal law. Employees who went on strike, or threatened to do so, risked criminal prosecution for such offences as

11

obstruction, molestation, intimidation and conspiracy. The turning point came in the 1870s with a series of statutes which effectively protected from criminal prosecution those who took part in, or organised, industrial action consisting of going on strike in breach of contracts. The most important of these were the Trade Union Act 1871 and the Conspiracy and Protection of Property Act 1875.

40. The Trade Union Act 1871 protected trade unions and their members from the consequences of the common law doctrine concerning "restraint of trade". Under the common law it is considered unlawful that unreasonable obstructions should be placed in the way of trade, and this includes trade in labour as well as in commodities. As a result, at common law the purposes of trade unions were regarded as unlawful for being "in restraint of trade". Before 1871 this had serious consequences, particularly for individual trade union members who, by taking part in trade union activities, could be exposed to the risk of prosecution for criminal conspiracy. Section 2 of the Trade Union Act sought to remove that risk by providing that:

"The purposes of any trade union should not, by reason merely that they are in restraint of trade, be deemed to be unlawful so as to render any member of such trade union liable to criminal prosecution for conspiracy or otherwise".

41. The Trade Union Act, however, provided only partial protection for trade union members and other employees from criminal prosecution for going on strike. Further protection was provided by the Conspiracy and Protection of Property Act three years later. The Act had three main effects:

(i) it provided that those who went on strike in a trade dispute were not to be indictable for criminal conspiracy unless, of course, they committed criminal acts like violence, damage to property, breach of the peace and so on;

(ii) it repealed previous statutes which made it a criminal offence in certain circumstances for manual workers to break their contracts of employment;

(iii) it made it clear that obstruction, molestation and intimidation could not be committed simply by virtue of threatening to go on strike; strikes were only illegal where they involved violence and the like or specific wrongful acts such as "watching and besetting" another person, hiding his tools and so on (this was in fact largely a re-enactment of the Criminal Law Amendment Act 1871).

42. The effect of these statutes was to reduce substantially the involvement of the criminal law in industrial disputes. As the Donovan Commission put it, "since then the criminal law has played a minor role in the regulation of trade disputes, although, of course, its provisions have to be observed. Very few people would now seriously suggest repealing these immunities or going back to the pre-1875 position where strikers are liable for criminal prosecution. When people talk about restricting trade union immunities today, they are very rarely thinking of the immunities from criminal liability".

12

43. The 1875 Act was a landmark in labour law. It remains of considerable interest because, in the protection it provided against prosecution for criminal liability, it is the first example of legal immunity for those involved in trade disputes. The Act said in effect that those who combined or agreed together to do something in a trade dispute were not to be liable for the offence of criminal conspiracy. It did not abolish the offence itself. It simply specified that a person was not to be liable for legal action if he committed that offence in specified circumstances. Those circumstances were defined in the Act as being when a person was acting "in contemplation of furtherance of a trade dispute". This phrase, which has sometimes been described as the "golden formula", became an integral part of subsequent immunities.

Development of civil law liabilities

44. From the 1890s onwards trade unions found their activities increasingly at risk from the civil law. This derived from a series of important judgements in the courts between 1890 and 1906. As a result, while not subject to the criminal penalties of fines or imprisonment, those organising and taking industrial action could now be sued for damages in tort (ie for a civil wrong other than a breach of contract) by those who were damaged by such action.

Liability in tort

45. As a result of these judgements at the turn of the century it seemed that the civil liabilities of strikers and strike organisers were developing in two ways:

   (i) first, and most important at the time, there was a new *civil liability for conspiracy*, the effect of which was that anyone who joined with another in a strike for purposes which the courts regarded as illegitimate was liable to be sued for damages;

   (ii) secondly, it appeared that the organisers of industrial action might also be liable in tort for *inducing a breach of the contracts of employment* of those whom they called out on strike.

46. In short, it seemed that these new liabilities had put the law back almost to where it was before the 1870s. Though strike leaders could no longer be prosecuted for striking, they could be sued for an injunction or damages.

Trade union liability

47. The most important development after 1875, however, resulted from the House of Lords' decision in the case of *Taff Vale Railway Co v Amalgamated Society of Railway Servants* in 1901. The case arose from a strike in August 1900 on the Taff Vale Railway in South Wales. A signal-man who had led a movement for a pay rise was alleged to have been victimised by the company and the West of England organiser of the Amalgamated Society of Railway Servants organised a strike in his support. After intitial hesitation the national union declared the strike official and its general secretary was sent down to South Wales to help.

13

48. The union organised picketing at Cardiff to prevent the company bringing in "blackleg" labour. The company responded by seeking an injunction, the novel feature of which was that it was taken out against the union itself, as well as the individual organisers. On 5 September 1900, when the strike had already been settled, the High Court granted the injunction against the union and gave the go ahead for the union to be sued for damages. The case was fought to the House of Lords on the question of whether the union itself was liable. The Court of Appeal overturned the High Court's decision, but the House of Lords reinstated it. Giving judgement Lord Macnaughten said:

"Has the Legislature authorized the creation of numerous bodies of men capable of owning great wealth and acting by agents with absolutely no responsibility for the wrongs they may do to other persons by the use of that wealth and the employment of those agents? In my opinion, Parliament has done nothing of the kind. I cannot find anything in the Acts of 1871 and 1876[1] . . . from beginning to end, to warrant or suggest such a notion".

49. The action for damages itself was finally heard in December 1902. It was decided that the union should pay £23,000 in damages and costs. The total costs to the union of fighting the case, including the final award of damages, amounted to £42,000, almost two-thirds of the union's income for one year.

50. The decision was a surprise. No one had previously thought that a union could be sued for damages in its own name for acts done by its officials. The cases in the 1890s had all seemed to indicate that the union itself was protected by virtue of the 1871 Act.

51. The decision produced an immediate protest from the trade unions and a demand for legislation. A trade union sponsored Bill was introduced into the House of Commons in 1903. It sought to protect unions from action for damages only when the industrial action was unofficial. If it could be shown that the "member or members . . . acted with the directly expressed sanction of the rules", then the union itself could be sued.

52. The Bill was defeated and this, coupled with union surprise at the size of the damages finally awarded in the Taff Vale case at the end of 1902, increased TUC fears about the extent of the risk to union funds. At the September Congress in 1903, a motion was passed committing the TUC to seek complete immunity for trade union funds.

53. The Taff Vale case has assumed a symbolic and psychological significance which is still very potent today. Trade unions have come to regard the House of Lords' decision as the moment when the whole development of the trade union movement was in greatest danger.

---

[1] The Trade Union Act 1871, and the Trade Union Amendment Act 1876.

Trade Disputes Act 1906—the foundation of modern immunity

54. The Conservative Government's response to trade union pressure for legislation in 1903 was to set up a Royal Commission "to inquire into the subject of disputes and Trade Combinations, and as to the law affecting them . . ." By the time it reported, however, at the beginning of 1906 a new Liberal Government had come to power already committed to trade union reform.

55. The result was the Trade Disputes Act 1906 which established the basis of the present immunity from action in tort for acts done in contemplation or furtherance of a trade dispute. It was in two main parts.

56. First, Sections 1 and 3 provided immunity from the new tort liabilities, (which are described in paragraphs 45 and 46 above) for acts done by a person in contemplation or furtherance of a trade dispute (which was defined in Section 5(3)):

- Section 1 provided protection against liability for civil conspiracy;
- Section 3 (first limb) provided immunity for a person who, in contemplation or furtherance of a trade dispute, induced another person to break a contract of employment (this did not appear in the original Bill as published but was added by an amendment in Committee proposed by Sir Charles Dilke);
- Section 3 (second limb) provided immunity against a possible tort of interference with trade, business or employment of another person.

57. Secondly, Section 4 provided that an action in tort could not be brought against a trade union for acts by its members or officials even though carried out on its behalf.[1] In other words, trade unions as such were given complete immunity from actions in tort and could not be sued for damages as they had been in the Taff Vale case.[2]

58. The Act followed closely the recommendations of the majority report of the Royal Commission except on the question of the immunity for trade union funds. The Commission had recommended only that unions should be able to protect themselves from the unofficial acts of their members and that the benefit funds of unions should be separated from the trade funds and made immune from liability. The Liberal Government's original Bill went no further than this. But, under pressure from the trade unions and from their growing number of representatives in Parliament, the Government agreed to amend the Bill to give unions the complete immunity they wanted. It was in this form that the Bill finally passed through both Houses of Parliament without a division on Second or Third Reading.

59. With two exceptions, which will be described below, the 1906 Act established the basic framework of immunities within which the law in relation to industrial action has operated for the last 75 years. Though the

---

[1] There were some minor exceptions in Section 4 relating to the liability of trustees of trade unions in connection with matters touching or concerning union property.
[2] In addition Section 2 of the 1906 Act (extending the provision in Section 7 of the 1875 Act) contained the first description of lawful picketing.

15

Act was repealed in 1971, its provisions are the basis for the Trade Union and Labour Relations Act 1974 and for the amendments to that made in 1976 and 1980.

The Trade Disputes and Trade Unions Act 1927

60. A partial departure from the immunities approach was made by the Trade Disputes and Trade Unions Act 1927 which was passed in the aftermath of the 1926 General Strike when the morale and prestige of trade unions was at a low ebb. The main effect of the Act was to make it a criminal offence to incite a strike which:

(a) had any object other than, or in addition to, the furtherance of a trade dispute within the trade or industry in which the strikers were engaged; and

(b) was a strike designed or calculated to coerce the Government either directly or by inflicting hardship upon the community.

The maximum penalty for inciting such a strike was two years imprisonment.

61. The 1927 Act also removed the protection conferred by the Trade Disputes Act 1906 from any act done in contemplation or furtherance of a strike declared illegal by the 1927 Act. Moreover, any person who refused to take part in a strike declared illegal could not, by virtue of the 1927 Act, be subject to expulsion from his union, to a fine or penalty or to deprivation of rights or benefits; or be liable to be placed under a disability or disadvantage as compared with other members of his union. Following the return of a Labour Government to power in 1945, the Act was repealed.

Judicial developments in the 1950s and 1960s

62. The 1927 Act did not repeal the Trade Disputes Act 1906 and until the 1950s the 1906 Act operated with a wide measure of acceptance. There were a number of important cases which affected certain aspects of the immunities established in 1906 but, on the whole, the period is notable for a relative absence of judicial interpretation. From 1952 onwards, however, a series of cases saw the further development of common law liabilities which the 1906 Act had not anticipated. Of these, two were of particular importance:

- the development of the indirect form of the tort of inducing a breach of contract; and

- the development of liability for the tort of intimidation.

Direct and indirect inducement to break a contract

63. The further development of the tort of inducing a breach of contract began in 1952 in the case of *Thomson v Deakin*. It was subsequently confirmed by judgements in a series of cases in the mid-1960s and early 1970s, including the House of Lords' judgement in the important case of *Stratford v Lindley*.

64. The effect of these judgements was to draw a distinction between direct and indirect inducement to break a contract and thus to raise questions about the extent of the immunity provided by the 1906 Act for inducing a breach of contract of employment. The Act had given no immunity for inducing a breach of *commercial* contract. If the union official went to the employer and persuaded him to break his commercial contract with another employer, that was direct inducement to break a commercial contract and was unlawful in itself, so it had no immunity under the 1906 Act.

65. The question which now arose was what if a union official called a strike of the employer's workers which caused the employer to break his commercial contracts with a customer? The 1906 Act clearly protected him in respect of the inducement to break a contract of employment which the strike call necessarily involved; but did it also protect the *indirect* inducement to break a commercial contract brought about by the inducement to break the contract of employment—the form of the tort which requires the use of unlawful means? In other words, was inducing a breach of contract of employment, which was declared not to be actionable by the 1906 Act, a lawful means of inducing the breach of a commercial contract? If it were lawful then there would be immunity for the action: if it were unlawful, then the organiser would be liable to be sued for inducing a breach of commercial contract. There were a number of conflicting judicial utterances on this question in the period before the passing of the Industrial Relations Act 1971 and it was only finally dealt with in the statutes of 1974 and 1976 which provided immunity for both direct and indirect inducement to break contracts.

66. A subsidiary question was whether the actual breach of a contract of employment (as opposed to the inducement) constituted an unlawful means of inducing the breach of a commercial contract. Following the case of *Rookes v Barnard* (see below) it seemed that it might.

Intimidation

67. The other important judicial development in the 1960s concerned the tort of intimidation. In 1964 in the case of *Rookes v Barnard* the House of Lords decided that a threat by three union officials that there would be a strike at BOAC if a non-unionist, Mr Rookes, were not removed from employment constituted unlawful conspiracy to commit the tort of intimidation. The Law Lords decided unanimously that a breach of contract was an unlawful act for the purpose of the tort of intimidation and that there was no difference between a threat to break a contract of employment and a threat of violence or other illegal act, which was what normally constituted intimidation. There was no protection under Section 3 of the 1906 Act because that only covered *actual* inducement to break a contract of employment and not the *threat* to do so.

68. As a result, it seemed possible that whenever a trade union official threatened a strike he might be liable to be sued for intimidation. Counsel for the defendants in the case described the decision as driving a "coach

17

and four" through the Trade Disputes Act 1906. Professor Kahn-Freund, one of the foremost authorities of the time on labour law, described it as a "frontal attack upon the right to strike". The TUC made strong representations to the Government.

69. The Trade Disputes Act 1965, introduced for the purpose by the newly elected Labour Government, extended immunity to cover this situation. It provided that an act done by a person in contemplation or furtherance of a trade dispute should not be actionable in tort on the ground only that it consisted in threatening that a contract of employment (whether one to which he is a party or not) would be broken, or that it would induce another person to break a contract of employment to which that person was a party. The Donovan Commission described the 1965 Act as "necessary for the protection of trade union officials in the reasonable performance of their functions".

The Donovan Commission

70. By the mid-1960s there was a widespread feeling that both the practice and law of British industrial relations needed an overhaul. In response, the new Labour Government established a Royal Commission on trade unions and employers' associations under the chairmanship of Lord Donovan.

71. The Commission reported in 1968. Apart from notes of dissent on specific points it was unanimous. The report's detailed recommendations will be discussed, where they are relevant, in the next chapter. In general, its analysis of the informal nature of plant level bargaining and of the growing incidence of disruptive unofficial and unconstitutional strikes was widely accepted and is still regarded as authoritative today. But the report's preference for largely voluntary reform, relying on unions and management voluntarily to bring about the necessary changes, received a mixed reaction.

72. The report's main conclusion on the 1906 immunities was not that they were too narrow or too wide but that, as a result of judicial interpretation, they constituted a legal maze.

"In the result the law has become complicated and irrational . . . Seeing that it is possible in the existing state of the law for trade unions or other persons to take action leading to breach of commercial contract without incurring any liability for damages, and that such liability is incurred only if a complicated state of the law is either unappreciated or misunderstood, the straightforward course appears to us to be that the law should be clarified and simplified: so that liability in achieving an end which the law regards as legitimate is not avoided or incurred according to whether a legal maze is successfully threaded or not". (Paragraphs 890 and 893).

The report recommended that one of the ways the law could be clarified was by extending the immunity for inducing a breach of a contract of employment to all contracts[1].

---

[1] Though a majority of the Commission thought this should apply only to officials of unions registered as proposed in another Commission recommendation.

"In Place of Strife"

73. The subsequent White Paper, "In Place of Strife", published by the Labour Government at the beginning of 1969, accepted this proposal. The controversy which the White Paper provoked centred on its other proposals: for the resolution of recognition disputes between unions; for union registration; for compulsory ballots in the case of official strikes; and for a statutory "conciliation pause" in the case of unconstitutional stoppages undertaken in breach of procedure. In each case there was to be provision for the Secretary of State for Employment to refer cases to a new Industrial Board and for financial penalties to be imposed on trade unions, employers and individuals for refusing to abide by its orders.

74. The proposals, particularly those involving fines on unions, were greeted by the trade unions with universal hostility. In the end the Government withdrew its proposals in return for a "solemn and binding" undertaking by the TUC that it would intervene in unofficial and unconstitutional strikes. A much truncated Industrial Relations Bill, shorn of all its penal clauses, was introduced just before the 1970 General Election which returned a Conservative Government to power.

The Industrial Relations Act 1971

75. The new Conservative Government embarked on the most sweeping and far reaching changes to industrial relations law ever attempted in Great Britain. These were embodied in the Industrial Relations Act 1971.

76. The Act repealed the Trade Disputes Act 1906. Though it then re-enacted the main immunities, extended to cover inducement to break all contracts as recommended by the Donovan Commission, the intention was not to widen the immunities, but rather to set aside the common law remedies available in tort in the ordinary courts in cases of industrial action. In their place the Act set up a new framework of industrial law. This included the creation of a new kind of "industrial tort", the unfair industrial practice, and a new court, the National Industrial Relations Court (NIRC), to adjudicate on the Act's provisions. There was also established a Commission for Industrial Relations with advisory and conciliation functions.

77. The Act placed a number of restrictions on industrial action, breach of which made the organisers of the action liable to be sued for unfair industrial practice. Some of these restrictions are discussed in more detail in the next chapter. As it turned out, however, the most important restriction was that contained in Section 96 of the Act. This made it an unfair industrial practice for anyone to induce or threaten to induce a breach of any contract unless he did so in contemplation or furtherance of a trade dispute and with the authority, or on behalf of, a registered trade union or employers' association. The Section was thus aimed specifically at unofficial action which the Donovan Commission had distinguished as particularly disruptive.

78. Under that Section, official action could only be taken by, or on the express authority of, a union registered under the provisions of the

Act. Registration was not to be compulsory but it carried with it a number of other privileges, including certain tax benefits. In order to retain registration, union rules had to meet certain requirements laid down in the Act. The rules were to include provisions to make clear the lines of authority within the union, particularly with regard to the calling of industrial action.

79. Both before and after it became law the 1971 Act encountered fierce opposition. The TUC led an immediate campaign to make its provisions unworkable. This consisted in instructing member unions not to register under the Act and in expelling those which did; and in refusing to recognise or cooperate with any of the institutions set up under the Act, including the National Industrial Relations Court. The provisions of the Act were put to two major tests: in the docks in 1972 and in the engineering industry in 1973–74. The TUC was not long able to sustain its campaign of total noncooperation with, and non-recognition of, the Court, but the operation of the Act was overshadowed by the fact that it led fairly swiftly to the imprisonment of individual workers and a growing anxiety about the extent to which its provisions could be operated in practice. Conflicting judicial decisions led to additional uncertainty. It is, however, not possible to make any final judgement about the likely long-term effectiveness of the Act because it was repealed in 1974.

80. The cases in the docks all involved the campaign by unofficial committees of dockers, composed largely of Transport and General Workers Union (TGWU) members, against the threat to their jobs posed by containerisation. Three cases came before the NIRC:

(i) In the first, a number of blacked road haulage firms in Liverpool and Hull, led by Heatons Transport Limited, successfully sought an injunction against the TGWU under Section 96 of the Act. The NIRC decided that the union itself was responsible for the blacking by the unofficial committees of dockers and, since it had failed to register under the Act, that it was unprotected by Section 96. In line with the TUC's campaign not to recognise the NIRC, the union initially refused to appear in court or to obey the injunction. It was fined first £5,000 and then £50,000 for disobedience of the orders of the court. This caused the TUC to revise its policy of noncooperation and to allow unions to appear to defend themselves. The TGWU then decided to pay the fine and to appeal the case to the Court of Appeal, claiming that it had tried to enforce the order that the blacking should cease but could not secure the cooperation of its members. The case was argued to the House of Lords on the question of whether the union or only the local dockers' leaders were liable. The original decision of the NIRC was upheld[1] (see (iii) below).

(ii) In the second case (Churchman and Others v Port of London Joint Shop Stewards Committee and Others [1972]) TGWU dockers picketed a container depot at Chobham Farm in London. The depot

---

[1] The implication of the Heatons case for the question of whether the union or its individual members were liable under Section 96 of the Act are dealt with more fully in paragraphs 117 to 122.

workers applied for and obtained an injunction against three individual pickets. When the picketing continued the three pickets were at risk of imprisonment for contempt of court if they did not appear before the NIRC. Dockers at five ports immediately went on sympathetic strike. A national strike was only averted by an appeal from the Official Solicitor on the dockers' behalf that there was not enough evidence to prove that they had broken the injunction. As a result the threat of imprisonment was withdrawn.

(iii) Finally, another container company affected by picketing and blacking, Midland Cold Storage Limited, brought an action under Section 96 against seven dockers. When five of them ignored the injunction they were imprisoned for contempt of court. There was an immediate national strike in the docks and a sympathy strike by workers in many other industries. The TUC also called a one day general strike. In the meantime, however, the House of Lords in the Heatons case had reversed the Court of Appeal decision and decided that, after all, the union was to be held financially responsible for the actions of its unofficial committees. The NIRC subsequently released the five dockers from imprisonment on the basis that primary relief should be sought against a union.

81. The second major test of the Act's industrial action provisions concerned a small engineering company, Con-Mech, which in September 1973 was involved in a recognition dispute with the Amalgamated Union of Engineering Workers (AUEW). There was a strike and picketing by AUEW members at the firm. An order banning the strike while the Commission for Industrial Relations investigated the case for recognition was ignored by the union. It was fined £75,000 for contempt and £100,000 of the union's assets were sequestrated. The AUEW's failure to register under the Act meant that the NIRC's subsequent recommendation that the union should be recognised could not be enforced and the company ignored it. It also sued the union for damages and in April 1974 was awarded £47,000 compensation. When the union refused to pay, the NIRC ordered the seizure of all its assets. The union, which had not defended the action at any stage, called a national strike but then called it off after the NIRC had accepted an offer from a group of anonymous donors to pay the fines and compensation owed by the AUEW.

The Trade Union and Labour Relations Acts 1974 and 1976

82. The Labour Government, elected in February 1974, came to power committed to repealing the Industrial Relations Act. This it did in the Trade Union and Labour Relations Act 1974.

83. The Act returned to the system of immunities which the 1971 Act had sought to replace. Section 13 provided individuals with the basic immunity from liability for civil conspiracy, inducement to break a contract of employment and interference with business, trade or employment, which had originally been provided by Sections 1 and 3 of the 1906 Act. But it also tried to deal with the consequences of the judicial decisions of the 1950s and 1960s by re-enacting the Trade Disputes Act 1965 and by declaring that inducement to break a contract of employment and an actual breach

21

of contract were not to be regarded as "unlawful means" for the purpose of establishing liabilities in tort.

84. In addition, Section 14 re-enacted the immunity in tort for trade union funds in a clearer and slightly more extended form than Section 4 of the 1906 Act. Section 29 re-enacted and, in some respects, extended the definition of "trade dispute" originally contained in the 1906 Act[1].

85. The most controversial aspect of the 1974 Act concerned Section 13. The intention of the Labour Government was to extend the immunity to inducement to break all contracts. However, because the Government had no overall majority in the House of Commons, it was unable to get Parliamentary approval for this proposal. Section 13, therefore, gave immunity only to inducement to break a contract of employment. This immunity was later extended to all contracts by the Trade Union and Labour Relations (Amendment) Act 1976. The Bill had been resisted by the Opposition in Parliament, and particularly in the House of Lords during 1975, and was only passed in 1976 when the Labour Government took steps to invoke the Parliament Acts 1911 and 1949.

In contemplation or furtherance of a trade dispute

86. A great deal of the argument between Government and Opposition in 1974 to 1976 centred on the likely effects of extending immunity to inducement to break all contracts. The Government claimed that the change was necessary simply to clarify the law. The Conservative Opposition was advised and asserted that it marked a significant extension of immunity which, in effect, licensed all industrial action even if it were directed against those far removed from the original dispute.

87. Subsequently the extent of the immunity established by the 1974 and 1976 Acts was limited by the Court of Appeal's interpretation of the so-called golden formula "in contemplation or furtherance of a trade dispute". In several cases the court granted an injunction against the organisers of the industrial action on the basis that it was not in furtherance of a trade dispute. There were two main strands to their thinking:

(a) that some action was too remote[1] from the main action to be arguably in furtherance of it; and

(b) that some action, wherever it took place, was not capable per se of furthering the main action.

88. One of the cases, *Express Newspapers v MacShane*, was, however, taken to the House of Lords. The case arose from a strike of journalists on provincial newspapers. To make the strike more effective the National

---

[1] This is discussed fully in paragraphs 182-187.

[1] As expounded in *Beaverbrook Newspapers v Keys* [1978], where Lord Denning MR held that "you cannot chase consequence after consequence after consequence in a long chain and say everything that follows a trade dispute is in 'furtherance' of it".

Union of Journalists (NUJ) ordered its members at the Press Association first to black news going to the provincial newspapers and then to come out on strike. Only half of the Press Association's workers did so. The NUJ then ordered its members at national newspapers, including the Daily Express, not to handle material from the Press Association. Express Newspapers sought an injunction against the General Secretary of the NUJ. The Court of Appeal, upholding the decision of the High Court, decided that for an act to be in furtherance of a trade dispute it must be reasonably capable of furthering the original dispute. It was not enough that the NUJ genuinely believed that the action at the Daily Express would further the dispute. The test of capability contained an objective element on which the NUJ in this case had failed to satisfy the courts.

89. When the case reached the House of Lords, however, in late 1979, the Court of Appeal's decision and its interpretation of the 1976 immunity was overturned. Four of the Law Lords found that the test of "in furtherance" is subjective (ie that it is a sufficient defence to show that the person doing the act complained of genuinely believes that it may further the trade dispute), though in each case discretion for "objective" correction by the court is left if the belief of the person organising the industrial action is obviously unreasonable. The fifth was of the opinion that there is an "objective" element in "in furtherance" which the court must appraise, but suggested that the court would be reluctant to substitute its own judgement for the judgement of experienced trade union leaders initiating the action.

90. The practical effect of the House of Lords' judgement was to prevent the courts from applying criteria of "remoteness" or "capability" in order to decide whether an act was in furtherance of a trade dispute. The courts still had to establish whether a trade dispute exists according to the definition in Section 29 of the Trade Union and Labour Relations Acts 1974 and 1976. But the court may not substitute its own opinion where a person claims that he has acted in furtherance of such a dispute, unless the court has cause to believe that the claim is not genuine. (This was re-affirmed in the House of Lords' judgement in the subsequent case of *Duport Steel v Sirs*). In other words, the House of Lords' judgement in the MacShane case confirmed the worst fears of those who opposed the extension of immunity to all contracts in 1974 and 1976. It now appeared that the law provided immunity for those who organised industrial action against companies far removed from the original dispute.

The Employment Act 1980

91. By the time the House of Lords had given judgement in the MacShane case in December 1979, the present Government had already published its Employment Bill which contained proposals to restrict immunity as regards secondary picketing. As a result of the judgement, the Government held immediate consultations and at Report Stage in the House of Commons added a further clause to the Bill to restrict the immunity for secondary action. It also promised to continue with its full review of immunities and to produce this Green Paper to promote further discussion.

23

92. The Employment Act 1980, which received Royal Assent on 1 August, restricts the immunity conferred by Section 13 of the Trade Union and Labour Relations Acts 1974 and 1976 in three ways:

(i) Section 16 provides that the immunity does not apply to an act done in the course of picketing unless that picketing is carried out at the picket's own place of work;

(ii) Section 17 provides that the immunity does not apply to secondary industrial action generally unless that action is undertaken by employees of customers or suppliers of the employer in dispute, its principal purpose is to interfere with the supply of goods or services between the employer in dispute and those customers and suppliers during the dispute, and it is reasonably likely to achieve that purpose;

(iii) Section 18 provides that the immunity does not apply where a person induces an employee of one employer to break his contract of employment in order to compel workers of another employer to join a particular trade union unless they are working at the same place. This provision was intended to halt the coercive recruitment tactics used by SLADE (see paragraphs 283–285).

The Employment Act does not change the Section 14 immunity for trade unions, nor the definition of trade dispute in Section 29.

The present position

93. To sum up, the present law governing collective industrial action remains based on a system of legal immunities. These immunities protect those who organise industrial action from liability for the criminal offences and civil wrongs for which the act of calling people out on strike in breach of contract would otherwise make them liable at common law. The immunities do not abolish the offences and wrongs against which they provide protection. Rather they remove liability in the circumstances of a trade dispute. To the extent to which these immunities are reduced, therefore, the common law liabilities are immediately restored. If they were repealed altogether, then trade unions and individuals would be at risk of legal action every time they organised a strike.

94. The present debate about immunities centres largely on the immunities from civil actions first provided by the Trade Disputes Act 1906. These are now contained in the Trade Union and Labour Relations Acts 1974 and 1976 and in the Employment Act 1980:

● Section 13 of the Trade Union and Labour Relations Act 1974 provides immunity from actions in tort for individuals who call or organise industrial action and in doing so interfere with contracts. The immunity applies only if there is a trade dispute (defined in Section 29 of the Act) and if the action is taken "in contemplation or furtherance of a trade dispute". For an act to be "in furtherance of a trade dispute", the person doing it must genuinely believe that it will further the dispute.

● Sections 16, 17 and 18 of the Employment Act 1980 have removed this immunity from specific kinds of industrial action. There remains wide immunity for those who organise *primary industrial action*. But

24

100. Secondly, there has been increasing criticism of the *complexity of* a legal system based on immunities. It has been argued that immunities are not easy to relate to the realities of industrial action; that they do not provide a sufficiently precise or comprehensive definition of the limits of lawful industrial action; and that throughout their history they have left too much scope for interpretation by the courts. This Chapter has shown how the immunities have developed in response to the common law liabilities which those organising industrial action would otherwise incur. As a result the language and concepts of the law relating to collective industrial action are not the language and concepts of industrial relations.

101. Most other countries have as the basis of their industrial relations law some form of "positive right" to strike or to organise in trade unions or to bargain collectively. Often these rights are set out in a written Constitution. It is sometimes suggested that the criticisms levelled at the present law would be met if the British system of immunities from actions in tort could be converted into a system of positive rights. Chapter 4 examines the questions which would need to be considered in converting the present system of legal immunities into a system based on the positive right to strike.

CHAPTER 3

POSSIBLE CHANGES TO THE PRESENT LAW ON IMMUNITIES

102. This Chapter considers possible changes to the existing framework of industrial relations law. It is concerned with the scope and extent of the immunities which the law now confers on the organiser of industrial action.

103. Section A considers whether the immunity in tort of trade unions themselves (conferred by Section 14 of the 1974 Act) should be brought into line with the immunity (conferred by Section 13) for individuals who organise industrial action. The remaining sections are concerned with possible limitations of either or both the Section 13 and 14 immunities in relation to particular issues viz secondary industrial action (B), picketing (C), the definition of a trade dispute (D), legally enforceable collective agreements (E), the holding of secret ballots before industrial action is taken (F), the closed shop and union membership issues (G) and the protection of the community in national emergencies (H). Many of these issues are closely inter-related. Changes in the law affecting some could have considerable implications for others. Individual proposals for changing the law need, therefore, to be considered not only on their merits but also in relation to the law on immunities as a whole.

A THE IMMUNITY FOR TRADE UNION FUNDS

104. Chapter 2 described how, since the Trade Disputes Act 1906, trade unions as such have had a more comprehensive immunity than that conferred upon their officials and other persons acting in contemplation or furtherance of a trade dispute. This immunity is now contained in Section 14 of the Trade Union and Labour Relations Act 1974. It was unaffected by the changes to the law on immunities made by the Employment Act 1980.

105. Section 14 gives immunity to trade unions from actions in tort (with certain minor exceptions[1]) for *all* acts, whether or not they are done in contemplation or furtherance of a trade dispute. It thereby prevents trade unions, as opposed to individuals, from being sued in tort for an injuction or damages either for their own acts or, more important, for acts done on their behalf by their officials or members.

106. The immunity therefore differs in two important respects from that conferred on individuals by Section 13 of the Trade Union and Labour Relations Acts 1974 and 1976:

- first, it applies to *all* torts (eg nuisance or negligence) and not simply to those involving interference with contracts specified in Section 13; and

---

[1] Under Section 14(2), a trade union is liable to be sued in tort for negligence, nuisance or breach of duty resulting in personal injury or for breach of duty relating to the ownership, occupation, possession, control or use of any property, where the act is not done in contemplation or furtherance of a trade dispute.

27

- secondly, it is not limited by the formula "in contemplation or furtherance of a trade dispute" and so extends to torts committed by trade
unions outside trade disputes.

In this way the law gives to British trade unions a status for which there
is no parallel in other countries.

107. If Section 14 were removed altogether trade unions would still be
protected by Section 13 and would, therefore, have the same immunity
as a person for acts done in contemplation or furtherance of a trade dispute[1].
Without the sort of immunity conferred by Section 13 it would be impossible
for trade unions to operate without a constant and potentially destructive
threat to their existence from actions for damages such as there was
between 1901 and 1906. But how far is the wider immunity for trade unions
provided by Section 14 necessary to enable trade unions effectively to represent the interests of their members?

How wide should the immunity for trade union funds be?

108. The legislators of 1906 believed that the House of Lords' judgement
in the Taff Vale case of 1901 had threatened the very existence of the
trade union movement by putting trade union funds at risk as a result of
almost any industrial action undertaken by their officials or members. They
decided that so unacceptable a threat could only be avoided by conferring
on trade unions an immunity from virtually all actions in tort.

109. Looking at the extent of this immunity in 1968, the Donovan Commission recommended that it should be limited to "torts committed in contemplation or furtherance of a trade dispute". It commented:

"Whatever may happen in a trade dispute, it is not the case that trade
unions frequently commit torts when no trade dispute is involved, or
that they need to do so. Their officials remain liable at all times to
be sued for any torts they commit: and when these are committed
while acting in the course of their employment as trade union officials
the union sometimes pays any damages which may be awarded out
of its own funds. To that extent the immunity conferred by Section
4(1) [of the 1906 Act: now S.14(1) of the 1974 Act] is waived..."
(paragraph 908)

"In all the circumstances we think it would be right and proper to
confine the immunity of trade unions so that it applies as regards torts
committed *in contemplation or furtherance of a trade dispute* but not
as regards any other tort..." (paragraph 909) (our italics)

110. However, the reasons adduced by the Commission for amending
the immunity in this way make it clear that they regarded the practical
effect of such a change as very limited. Since trade unions have not sought

---

[1] This is because Section 13 confers immunity on "any person" which, in legal terms, covers
an unincorporated body of persons such as a trade union as well as an individual: but to
ensure that trade unions were subject to Section 13, it might be necessary to have a declaratory
provision to this effect.

to avoid liability for torts committed outside a trade dispute, the withdrawal of the immunity from such torts would be little more than a recognition of existing practice.

111. In recent years interest has focused on the more radical suggestion of bringing the Section 14 immunity for trade unions fully into line with the Section 13 immunity for individuals. This would mean that a trade union itself could be sued for an injunction or damages and its funds would be at risk if the officials, or even members, of that trade union committed torts—for example organising secondary action beyond the limits laid down in Section 17 of the Employment Act 1980—for which there is no immunity under Section 13.

112. Four main arguments have been advanced for such a narrowing of the Section 14 immunity: first, that it is right in principle that trade unions should be held financially responsible for the unlawful acts of their officials; secondly, that if trade unions were made financially responsible in this way they could be expected in their own interest to exert greater internal discipline over their officials and members, particularly in respect of unofficial action; thirdly, that it would enable employers to gain proper redress from trade unions for damage done to them by unlawful industrial action, whereas at present they can only sue individuals who are not usually in a position to pay substantial damages; and finally, that it would remove the risk of individual trade unionists adopting the role of "martyrs" if they were sued for acting unlawfully in the course of an industrial dispute.

113. A number of arguments are advanced against such a narrowing of the Section 14 immunity: first, that because so much industrial action is unofficial it would often be uncertain whether trade unions could in fact be held to be legally responsible for the unlawful acts of their officials and members; secondly, that because of this uncertainty, bringing the Section 13 and Section 14 immunities into line would not itself be a significant deterrent to unlawful industrial action and that, for the same reason, it would not significantly reduce the risk of "martyrdom"; thirdly, that employers are in any case more concerned to get unlawful industrial action stopped quickly than to claim compensation for the damage it causes; and, finally, that because of the way British trade unions are organised and disputes arise, the effect of putting union funds at risk, far from making unions more disciplined organisations, would be to encourage internal dissension, to weaken their internal authority and therefore to threaten an increase in unofficial action.

114. The argument of principle has always been closely bound up with arguments of practical effect. As described in paragraphs 47–53 there was considerable controversy between 1901 and 1906 over the extent of the immunity trade unions needed and should be allowed. The immunity ultimately conferred by Section 4 of the 1906 Act was wider than that recommended by the Royal Commission which had been appointed to consider the whole subject following the Taff Vale case. It can be argued that it was unnecessary and anomalous from the outset for trade unions to have a wider immunity than their officials and that it has become more evidently

29

anomalous as the bargaining power of trade unions has increased. Against this it is argued that the immunity for trade unions, now contained in Section 14 of the 1974 Act, has acquired immense symbolic and psychological significance for the trade union movement so that the practical consequences of any change which put union funds at risk need to be weighed very carefully.

115. If the Section 13 and Section 14 immunities were brought into line, how likely is it that unions would be held liable for the unlawful actions of their officials or members? Would the trade unions do more to discipline their officials and members who took unlawful action if such action put union funds at risk? Would employers make use of the ability to seek compensation for the damage caused by unlawful action? These are the issues which are considered in the following paragraphs.

Vicarious liability[1]

116. It is not always easy to determine when any organisation is to be held legally responsible for action done on its behalf and it is particularly difficult to determine this in the case of unincorporated bodies such as trade unions. In general terms the law holds a person (which in this case includes a trade union) liable, not only for torts committed by himself, but—subject to certain conditions—for torts committed by persons acting or purporting to act on his behalf. Where the relationship of master and servant exists, as in the case of a union and its employees, the master is liable for the torts of the servant if—but only if—they are committed in the course of the servant's employment in the context of industrial action. In recent years, trade unions have been penalised as a result of this relationship only when they refused to register under the Industrial Relations Act 1971 thereby rendering themselves and their officials liable for an unfair industrial practice if, for example, in contemplation or furtherance of an industrial dispute, they induced or threatened a breach of contract. It was left to the courts to decide, using the common law concept of vicarious liability, when unions which had refused to register under the Act were responsible for acts done by their officials. The cases in which this issue was involved raised many questions and by the time the 1971 Act was repealed there was considerable uncertainty about when a trade union might or might not be held responsible for the actions of its officials.

117. The first case to reach the House of Lords was *Heatons Transport v TGWU*,[1] involving blacking at the Liverpool and Hull docks. In this case the House of Lords, unanimously overruling a unanimous Court of Appeal, established the vicarious liability of a union which was unregistered under the 1971 Act for "unfair industrial practices" committed by shop stewards acting within scope of a "general implied authority" to take industrial action at their workplace in furtherance of union policy which included the "blacking" of haulier firms. The authority of an official of a trade union,

---

[1] Vicarious liability means that one person takes the place of another so far as liability is concerned.

[1] See also paragraph 80.

including a shop steward, to bind the union was found to depend on two sources: the written rule book of the union and the custom and practice of the union. The House of Lords held that:

"If the authority to take a particular type of action is not excluded by the rules, and if such authority is reasonably to be implied from custom and practice, such authority will continue to exist until unequivocably withdrawn".

(The TGWU subsequently issued shop stewards with credentials which limited their authority in relation to organising industrial action). Moreover, in the same case the House of Lords ruled that it was not enough for a union to draw attention to a court order restraining the industrial action or to advise their members to desist. They should take some positive steps to stop the action, if necessary, withdrawing a shop steward's credentials to act on the union's behalf.

118. The case of Heatons involved issues, such as "implied authority" and "custom and practice", which were inherently imprecise. In another case which reached the House of Lords, *General Aviation Services (UK) Ltd v TGWU*, a majority of the House of Lords found that the circumstances of the Heatons case—particularly the local situation at the Liverpool and Hull docks and the evidence of a union policy on containerisation—were not repeated and that shop stewards at Heathrow airport were not acting with the authority of the defendant union.

119. No cases involving trade union liability for unlawful action by individual *members*, rather than officials, arose under the 1971 Act but of course such action—perhaps organised by self-appointed leaders—is far from unknown. Such cases would be likely to pose less difficulty for the courts: it seems improbable that they would hold a trade union responsible for action which was so clearly unauthorised.

120. The experience of the 1971 Act suggests that it would be unsatisfactory to remove the Section 14 immunity without attempting to deal specifically with the issue of vicarious responsibility. It would leave the courts a wide discretion if, as in 1971, only general principles were stated. For example, a requirement that trade unions should use their "best endeavours" to bring unlawful action by their officials and members to an end or to take "all reasonable steps" (the current Australian model[1]) would still leave the courts with the difficulty of determining what constituted "best endeavours" or "reasonable steps" in each case. It may be that a more particular definition would be required for a tolerable degree of accuracy to be achieved. But the problem is more than a matter of devising a satisfactory definition of vicarious liability. A definition which in its application compelled a trade union to expel members who had acted unlawfully in order to satisfy the courts that it had used its "best endeavours" to bring that unlawful action to an end could have very serious consequences for trade union authority and collective bargaining arrangements. The effect it can be argued might well be to strengthen the power of unofficial,

[1] See Appendix, paragraph 15.

31

127. Furthermore, some of the factors already noted might reduce the impact of a change in the law on trade unions. To the extent that it was necessary as a matter of justice for the law to continue to treat unofficial action as beyond the responsibility of trade unions (see paragraph 120), the existing pressures which lead unions to seek to control those taking such action could be reduced. To the extent that it was uncertain when the courts would and would not hold unions responsible for unlawful, unofficial action[1], trade unions might be inclined to avoid making any internal changes and to resist the application of the law, as they did between 1972 and 1974. The deep-rooted sensitivity of trade unions to any interference with their internal arrangements would tend to reinforce this inclination. Much would also depend on the view the trade unions took of the prospects of an early reinstatement of the previous immunity.

128. Opponents of change in the immunity for trade union funds argue that it is fallacious to assume that the trade unions could or would turn themselves into more authoritarian structures under the threat of having to pay out large sums in damages. In their view, the shift in the balance of power within trade unions to the shop floor has gone too far to be reversed by a change in the law. It is said that some of those who organise unofficial action at plant or shop floor level have come to have little or no regard for their union leaders at national level and would be unmoved by any threat to the central funds of their unions, not least because, while a strike is unofficial, a union's financial support is withheld. Thus the more likely effect of putting union funds at risk would be a further weakening of the authority of national leaders and even the breakdown or splintering of some unions under the threat, or as a result, of large scale expulsions. Far from reducing the incidence of unofficial action, they argue, the ultimate result might be to increase it. The existing system of industrial relations, whatever its many damaging imperfections, could be imperilled.

129. On the other hand, proponents of change point out that trade unions can, and in certain circumstances already do, exercise control over their members. They therefore argue that if the funds of trade unions were at risk they would find ways of safeguarding them by exerting greater control over their members. Britain is unique in the nature and extent of the immunity the law confers on trade unions as such and trade unions in other countries operate effectively within a framework of law under which they can be sued if their officials or members act unlawfully or in breach of a legally enforceable collective agreement. If trade unions were prepared to adjust their internal organisation so that they exercised greater control over their members the problems of deciding when a union was vicariously responsible for the acts of its members would be considerably reduced.

Nature and extent of damages

130. Another advantage claimed for the removal of the Section 14 immunity is that it would enable employers to sue trade unions for damages incurred as a result of unlawful industrial action. At present, it is argued,

---

[1] Trade unions would, of course, still have immunity in cases of unofficial action which was lawful under Section 13.

an employer has no prospect of gaining financial redress because he can only sue the individual organisers of unlawful action. This raises two issues:

- the amount of damages which might be available to an employer;
- the extent to which employers would wish to sue for damages.

131. Experience of cases which arose under the 1971 Act shows that, even in the smallest disputes, claims for damages can be very large. General Aviation Services Ltd, for example, in a localised dispute with the TGWU claimed damages of £2 million against the union. It would, of course, be possible to fix by legislation a limit on the amount of damages which could be awarded in a particular case: for example, by putting a ceiling on the damages which could be claimed by an individual employer or alternatively by all the employers involved in a particular dispute. Such a limit could be related to the size of a union's membership although this would necessarily be very arbitrary in effect. The experience of the 1971 Act (and, indeed, of the Taff Vale case) suggests that, without a limit of some kind, a union could be bankrupted by a relatively minor instance of unlawful industrial action. On the other hand, any arbitrary limit on the amount of damages might prevent an employer from gaining full compensation for the loss he had suffered as a result of unlawful action and would thus run counter to one of the purposes of narrowing the immunity.

132. Narrowing the Section 14 immunity for trade union funds would have little or no impact unless employers were prepared to sue trade unions for damages in cases of unlawful industrial action. Those who are opposed to a change in the Section 14 immunity argue that an employer's primary concern is to get industrial action stopped quickly and that an injunction to restrain the organiser of the unlawful action provides an effective means of achieving this. An action for damages against the union, which would often be heard long after the dispute was over, would once more sour industrial relations and might threaten continuing or renewed disruption.[1]

133. Between 1972 and 1974 only one out of the 33 applications by employers for relief from industrial action reached a full hearing of a complaint for damages. In that case (as described in paragraph 81) the AUEW was ordered to pay £47,000 compensation to the Con-Mech engineering company for losses resulting from the union's unfair industrial practices. The union refused to pay and the court ordered the sequestration of all its assets. When the AUEW then threatened to call a strike throughout the engineering industry, anonymous donors offered to discharge the union's liabilities. The court, while making clear that this did not involve any surrender of its authority, accepted the offer and the sequestrated funds were returned to the union. Employers' behaviour today might not be the same as in the early 1970s. Nevertheless, the experience of the operation of the 1971 Act must raise doubts about the extent to which employers might exercise a right to claim damages from unions.

---

[1] Even when the question of liability to pay damages has been decided in the courts, the assessment of the amount could take considerably longer. In the Taff Vale case (see paragraphs 49–53) damages were assessed a year after judgement was given in the House of Lords.

35

The "martyrdom" of individual union officials

134. In the event of unlawful industrial action—or the threat of it—the employer whose business has been, or may be, damaged is already able to bring civil proceedings against the union official (or unofficial leader) who is organising the action. The employer normally applies for an injunction requiring the official to call off the action. If the official refuses to obey an injunction he is liable for contempt and may be fined and ultimately, if the contempt continues, imprisoned. This procedure carries the risk that individuals may be moved to seek martyrdom by deliberately ignoring an injunction, with the risk that new and emotive grounds might then be provided to widen and prolong the dispute. It is sometimes argued that this risk could be reduced if Section 14 of the Trade Union and Labour Relations Act 1974 were amended to enable the courts to issue injunctions against the union itself and fine the union for non-observance of the injunction. In the event of the failure of the union to pay such a fine, the assets of the union might be sequestrated.

135. However, quite apart from the other Implications of removing the Section 14 immunity already discussed, it is far from certain that this procedure would be as effective as that which now exists or that it would significantly diminish the risks of self-inflicted martyrdom. It could be a less certain and speedy means of getting unlawful action stopped, particularly in the case of unofficial industrial action which is carried on without a union's authority or in defiance of its instructions. Certainly, where the courts held that a trade union was not responsible or that it had done all it could reasonably be expected to do to stop such unofficial action, the law would be powerless to help an injured employer if he could not then seek an injunction against the individual organising the unofficial action. In practice, if civil proceedings could be taken against both individuals and trade unions, it is likely that employers would seek injunctions against individuals where the unlawful action was unofficial and against both named union officials and the union itself where the unlawful action was official. In such circumstances, the opportunities for individuals to seek martyrdom might be reduced, but would not be eliminated.

Conclusion

136. Great Britain is unique in the extent of the immunity from legal action which it affords to trade unions as such. Whereas in most other countries the legal liability of trade unions is deeply rooted in the legal system and has shaped their growth and development, the trade unions in this country have grown up within a legal system which has since 1906 protected them from legal action for the unlawful acts of their members. Industrial relations have undergone great changes since the present immunity was introduced in 1906 and it must now be considered whether the extent of immunity then thought necessary to safeguard the existence and operation of trade unions is still appropriate 75 years later. In particular, it is often questioned whether the law should continue to provide trade unions with a wider immunity than it provides for individuals who organise industrial action. The arguments for and against bringing these immunities into line with each other go to the heart of the debate on the failings of

36

our industrial relations system and practices, and on the role the law can reasonably be expected to play in improving them. Consideration of these arguments has to take account of the movement of bargaining power to the shop floor and the implication of this development for the concept of "trade union power".

137. The Government would welcome views on the issues discussed in this Chapter. In particular, if the Section 14 immunity for trade unions were narrowed to bring it fully into line with the Section 13 immunity for individuals, thus putting union funds at risk for the unlawful acts of union officials and members:

  (a) would the change result in more responsible behaviour by trade unions themselves and by their officials and members?

  (b) to what extent would employers in practice make use of the ability to sue trade unions for injunctions and damages in cases of unlawful action?

B THE IMMUNITY FOR SECONDARY INDUSTRIAL ACTION

138. Another important issue in the debate about trade union immunities in recent years has been how far there should be immunity for secondary action against employers and employees not involved in a dispute. This question is examined below.

139. Secondary action generally means industrial action by employees of an employer who is not party to a trade dispute. It is usually taken either to make more effective an existing strike or simply to express support for employees who are in dispute with their employer. It can be undertaken spontaneously by employees on their own initiative, often attracting the term "sympathetic action", or, perhaps reluctantly, on instructions from the union. The issue in dispute might be held to involve a principle of general application to employees beyond the immediate disputants and, therefore, to be fought and defended by such employees; or a narrow domestic issue of little or no concern to employees of employers not in dispute.

140. The form of secondary action may be a strike or action short of a strike such as blacking goods or services going to or from the employer in dispute. It is also usually taken to include secondary picketing. Since, however, secondary picketing has been dealt with separately from other forms of secondary action in the Employment Act 1980 it is considered separately in this Green Paper. It is discussed below in Section C of this Chapter.

141. There is nothing new about secondary action. It has customarily been used by unions to put additional pressure on the employer in dispute to settle by sealing off his sources of supply and/or his outlet for sales. It has been particularly used where primary industrial action by the employees of the employer in dispute has proved ineffective. In recent

years, however, there have been disturbing signs that, with the growing strength of trade union organisation, secondary action is being used, not for its traditional purpose of putting commercial pressure on the employer in dispute, but indiscriminately, in both official and unofficial disputes, to spread the consequences of the dispute to as many people as possible, to inflict damage on the economy and to put pressure on the community as a whole.

142. This development received encouragement from the wide immunity for inducement to break *all* contracts which was conferred by the Trade Union and Labour Relations (Amendment) Act 1976. As was described in Chapter 2, it seemed at first that the Court of Appeal would limit the impact of that Act by applying tests of remoteness and capability to the words "in furtherance of a trade dispute". But the trend was reversed by the House of Lords in the case of *Express Newspapers v MacShane* in December 1979. The first major dispute following the judgement—the national steel strike of early 1980—was characterised by extensive secondary action including blocking by dockers, railwaymen and lorry drivers, and the calling out on strike of employees in the private steel sector who had no dispute with their employers and in many cases did not want to strike.

143. The Government took immediate action in the Employment Act to deal with the effects of the MacShane judgement. Under Section 17 of the Act if secondary action interferes with commercial contracts its organiser has no immunity unless:

(i) the secondary action is taken by employees of a supplier or customer of the employer in dispute and its principal purpose and likely effect is to prevent or disrupt supplies during the dispute going to or from the employer in dispute; or

(ii) the secondary action is taken by employees of an employer associated with an employer in dispute (or a supplier or customer to such an associated employer) to whom the employer in dispute has, because of the dispute, transferred work; and the principle purpose and likely effect of the secondary action is to disrupt the supply of goods or services which, but for the dispute, would have been supplied to or by the employer in dispute.

144. These provisions came into force on 8 September 1980. They were based on an assessment by the Government of what it was immediately necessary and practicable to do in response to the MacShane judgement. They sought to reconcile the need to protect businesses not involved in a dispute from the damaging effects of secondary action and the need to enable trade union officials to exert pressure in furtherance of their claims. Together with the sanction employers have always had of dismissing or disciplining employees who do not carry out their contracts of employment, these provisions provide a considerable disincentive to secondary action. During consultations and debates on the Employment Bill, however, views were strongly expressed that those not involved in a dispute need greater protection than the Act provides.

145. The main proposals for change are considered below. The basic question to be considered is how far, if at all, the law should provide immunity for those organising secondary action. On the one hand trade union solidarity and assistance to fellow workers has long been a feature of industrial disputes in Great Britain. On the other hand those who are not parties to a dispute (including other workers) are entitled to protection from reckless and indiscriminate interference with their businesses and livelihood. Sympathetic action has too often been used as the pretext for extending a strike or blacking to involve employees and employers who have no interest or connection with the original dispute. Its purpose can become simply to inflict maximum damage and the interests of those not involved in the dispute and the community as a whole can suffer severely. It is sometimes argued that there is point and purpose in secondary action only where the primary employer is still operating. However, except if the employer in dispute has sacked his unionised workers, this will normally mean that those taking the primary action cannot command the support of their own workmates. It is suggested that this argues for further abridgement of immunity for industrial action taken elsewhere in furtherance of a primary dispute.

146. This Section does not consider the possibility of *reducing* the protection for employers newly established by the Employment Act. There are those who argue that the Act went too far in restricting secondary action. In the Government's view, however, the 1976 Act, as interpreted by the House of Lords in the MacShane case, granted trade union officials and their members an unacceptably wide immunity which encouraged the spread of damaging secondary action. A return to that position cannot be contemplated.

Proposals for change

147. A number of proposals for restricting secondary action have been made.

(i) No immunity for secondary action

148. The most far-reaching proposal would be to remove immunity from all secondary action. This could be achieved in a number of ways. In essence it would mean removing all immunity for inducing breaches of contract from any person who organised industrial action by employees of an employer who was not himself in dispute. There would remain immunity only for organising action by employees who were in dispute with their own employer.

149. This would appear to be a clear restriction on immunity easily understood by all concerned and simply applied by the courts. It can be argued that it is the only limitation which would provide complete protection for those employers and employees whose companies are subjected to secondary action in support of a dispute in which they are not involved. Against this it can be argued that, in some cases, secondary action is the only means by which pressure can be brought on an employer in dispute, for example where the employer has sacked all his unionised employees; that

secondary action by fellow union members is a long standing trade union practice deeply based in concepts of unity and mutual assistance; and that it could tilt the balance of power unacceptably to the benefit of employers.

150. It has been argued that this proposal could be made less harsh if the right to sue in these circumstances were to be restored only to the employer not in dispute and were to be denied to the employer who is in dispute. Against this it can be said that, from the trade union official's point of view, it is immaterial whether he can be sued by the employer in dispute or not: it is the threat of being sued at all which matters. The official would still be at risk of legal action every time he organised a secondary strike or secondary blacking. Furthermore, there would always be the possibility of the employer in dispute arranging for the other employer to take legal action and promising to indemnify him against any adverse outcome.

(ii) Immunity for specific types of secondary action

151. Instead of removing immunity from all secondary action, another possibility would be to limit it closely to specific *types* of secondary action. Examples of circumstances in which it is argued that there should be immunity for secondary action are where no primary action is possible (eg because an employer has sacked all his unionised employees), or where a firm is providing goods to the employer in dispute in substitution for goods which the employees on strike would normally make.

152. Alternatively, or additionally, immunity could be limited to secondary action against an employer who is giving material support or assistance to the employer in dispute. The justification for this would be that, if an employer takes active steps to become involved in a dispute by deliberately providing assistance to the employer in dispute, then it is not unreasonable that he should be at risk from industrial action.

153. Those who argue for these approaches claim for them the advantage that they enable immunity to be given only in those very specific instances where it is generally agreed to be justified and not otherwise. On the other hand, these approaches are seen to involve difficulties of practical application. Circumstances surrounding disputes are often confused and motives are complex. There could well be protracted arguments in the courts about the interpretation of any provision on the lines discussed in paragraphs 151 and 152 above, involving industrial issues which, it is claimed, the courts are not well equipped to determine.

154. The concept of "material support" was employed in the Industrial Relations Act 1971. Section 98 provided that an employer was to be regarded as an extraneous party to a dispute, and therefore protected against secondary action, if he had not taken any action in material support of a party to the dispute. What constituted "material support", however, was not tested before the repeal of the Act and it remained a phrase of uncertain ambit. Section 98 said that a person was not to be regarded as having given material support merely because he was an associated employer of, or in

the same employers' association as, the employer in dispute, or because he had contributed to a relief fund, or supplied goods or services in pursuance of a contract into which the employer in dispute entered before the dispute began. But that still left the courts with the problem of determining what else "material support" might mean when these matters had been discounted.

(iii) Immunity for inducing breach of contract of employment

155. Another approach would be to limit the immunity for secondary action according to the type of contract involved. One such possibility would be to restrict the immunity to inducing a breach of a contract of employment.

156. The effects of this would be very uncertain. It was seen in Chapter 2 that judicial decisions in the 1950s and 1960s threw considerable doubt on the extent to which the 1906 immunity for inducing a breach of a contract of employment protected action which also interfered, as most industrial action inevitably does, with commercial contracts. To return to that position would raise many of those doubts again and, unless a way could be found of dealing with those doubts, it would be left to the courts in each instance to establish how far the immunity extended.

157. It is sometimes argued that the effect of restricting the immunity to contracts of employment would be to make unlawful all but primary action. But this is far from certain. It would depend on whether the immunity for interference with contracts of employment was construed as "lawful means" thus conferring immunity from interference with commercial contracts. If there were no immunity for any interference with commercial contracts then most industrial action, including primary action, would be at risk. If, however, the immunity for interference with contracts of employment covered indirect interference with commercial contracts by means of interfering with contracts of employment, then almost all industrial action, including most secondary action, might be permitted.

158. In short, restricting the immunity to interference with contracts of employment without clarifying in legislation the issues raised in paragraph 157 above, would result in a restoration of what the Donovan Commission described as a "legal maze" (see paragraph 72).

(iv) Immunity for interfering with the commercial contracts of the employer in dispute

159. Another proposal is that there should only be immunity for industrial action which interferes exclusively with the commercial contracts between the employer in dispute and his customers and suppliers, but not for industrial action which interferes with other commercial contracts to which the employer in dispute is not a party.

160. This would retain immunity for secondary action which was targeted very specifically on the commercial contracts of the employer in dispute. It would mean, for example, that there would be immunity for action by

employees of a supplier to an employer in dispute which was aimed at cutting off supplies to that employer. But if the action also cut off supplies to other employers not in dispute then there would be no immunity.

161. This, it is argued, would protect companies not in dispute against the damaging "spin-off" effects of secondary action: only the the employer in dispute and those with a commercial contract with him would be unprotected. It is claimed, on the other hand, that this approach would make secondary action virtually impossible. This is because it is rarely possible in practice for employees of a supplier or customer to take secondary action which affects *only* the contract with the employer in dispute. However accurately they seek to target their action, they will very often interfere with other contracts as an inevitable consequence. As an example, stopping supplies to the employer in dispute will almost always prevent the employer in dispute fulfilling his contracts with other employers. If this happens, then under this approach the secondary action would become unlawful.

Conclusion

162. Whatever the arguments for and against a particular option, the main judgement to be made is how far it is desirable and practicable to restrict the immunity for secondary action further than it has been restricted already by the Employment Act 1980. In making that judgement, conflicting considerations must be balanced.

163. On the one hand, there is a continuing need to provide effective protection for those not involved in a dispute against damaging secondary action, particularly against the kind of indiscriminate secondary action which has been a feature of some recent disputes. On the other hand, any changes must take account of the industrial reality that secondary action "to exert additional economic pressure on the employer in dispute by sealing off his sources of supply of materials or his outlets for sales or both . . ." is, to quote the Donovan Commission's words, "a familiar aspect of trade disputes". It also has a long and emotive history. With this in mind, any proposed change would need to be tested against its likely effectiveness and the consequences for industrial relations generally.

164. The Government would welcome views on these questions:

(i) what is the right balance between the need to protect third parties against secondary action and the need to ensure that trade unions and their officials have sufficient immunity to enable them to defend their members effectively?

(ii) what changes, if any, should there be in the restriction on secondary action established by Section 17 of the Employment Act 1980?

C PICKETING

165. The use of pickets in industrial disputes has been the subject of widespread and increasing public concern in recent years. One of the main purposes of the Employment Act 1980 was to withdraw the Section 13 immunity from those who picket except at their own place of work. This

Section considers suggestions which have been made for further strengthening the law on picketing.

The present law

166. Section 15 of the Trade Union and Labour Relations Act 1974, as amended by the Employment Act 1980, sets out the basic conditions for lawful industrial picketing:

(i) it must be undertaken in contemplation or furtherance of a trade dispute;

(ii) it must be carried out by a person attending at or near his own place of work;[1] or in the case of a trade union official at or near the place of work of a member of his union whom he is accompanying on the picket line and whom he represents; and

(iii) its only purpose must be peacefully obtaining or communicating information or peacefully persuading a person to work or not to work.

167. Picketing commonly involves persuading employees to break their contracts of employment by not going to work and, by disrupting the business of the employer who is being picketed, interfering with his commercial contracts with other employers. Provided that picketing satisfies the conditions described in paragraph 166, those who organise and engage in it are protected by Section 13 of the Trade Union and Labour Relations Acts 1974 and 1976 from being sued in the civil courts for these civil wrongs.

168. These provisions apply where employees are picketing at their own place of work in support of a dispute with their own employer. Where, however, employees picket at their own place of work in support of a dispute between another employer and his employees, such picketing must further satisfy the requirements of lawful secondary action in Section 17 of the Employment Act 1980 if it is to have the protection of the Section 13 immunity. In practice this means that these pickets have to target their picketing precisely on the supply of goods or services between their employer and the employer in dispute. If they try to impose an indiscriminate blockade on their employer's premises, they are liable to be sued in the civil courts.

169. A picket who commits a criminal offence is just as liable to prosecution as any other member of the public who breaks the law. The civil law immunities provided by Section 13 and Section 15 of the Trade Union and Labour Relations Act 1974 give no protection against prosecution for criminal offences.

---

[1] Section 15 of the 1974 Act, as amended by the Employment Act 1980, distinguishes two specific groups of employees:
    —those (eg mobile workers) who work at more than one place of work;
    —those for whom it is impracticable to picket at their own place of work because of its location.
It declares that it is lawful for such workers to picket those premises of their employer from which they work or from which their work is administered. Section 15 also declares that it is lawful for a dismissed worker to picket at his former place of work in connection with the dispute which has been the occasion of the dismissal.

43

Proposals for changes in the law

170. It has been suggested that the Section 13 immunity might be limited in respect of picketing to primary action alone. The consequence of this would be that strikers who were not in dispute with their own employer but, say, picketing in the course of a sympathetic (ie secondary) strike—even a lawful strike—would have no immunity in respect of picketing at all.

171. If all secondary action were made unlawful there would of course be a strong case for specifically withdrawing the immunity in respect of picketing in all circumstances except primary action. The arguments for and against such a restriction of secondary action generally are set out in Section B. It can be argued that it would be unrealistic to allow people to strike lawfully but not to picket their own place of work while they are on strike. On this view, picketing at the picket's own place of work in the course of secondary action should be subject only to whatever limitations the law places on the secondary action itself.[1]

172. It has also been suggested that employers who suffer loss as a result of picketing which is unlawful under the 1980 Act may have difficulty in securing effective redress by means of the existing injunctive procedures. Injunctions can be sought only against named individuals and it has been pointed out that in some circumstances an employer might have difficulty in ascertaining pickets' names. There is no obligation on the pickets to supply their names and addresses and, because the injunction is sought under the civil law, which the police have no responsibility for enforcing, the employer cannot enlist the help of the police for this purpose. This should not normally be a problem for the employer because an injunction can be sought against the picket organiser (who is normally readily identifiable) even if, as may be the case with a trade union official, he is not himself present on the picket line. Moreover, others deliberately aiding and abetting the named individual to disobey the injunction may be liable for contempt of court even if they are not themselves named in it.

173. However, it has been suggested that a faster and more certain procedure would be to place an obligation on the police to ascertain the names and addresses of pickets at the request of the employer concerned in these circumstances, and that it should be made a criminal offence for the pickets to refuse to supply their names and addresses.

174. The main objection is that this would involve a breach of what has hitherto been regarded as an important principle in relation to the conduct of picketing—namely the neutrality of the police. Provided that the pickets are peaceful and do not commit or threaten to commit criminal offences,

---

[1] That is, of course, the position under Section 17 of the Employment Act 1980 (see paragraph 168 above).

the police do not become involved: they are impartial as between employer and picket. Their role is to see that the peace is kept, not to take sides. The police themselves attach the greatest importance to maintaining this position of neutrality. It enables them in the great majority of cases to avoid hostility and establish reasonable relations with pickets. To require the police to demand names and addresses at the request of the employer might well be seen as enlisting their services on the side of the employer.

175. It has been suggested that an alternative approach might be to provide in the law for injunctions to be taken out against "the act of picketing" ie against unnamed persons. This, it is suggested, would also deal with the so-called rotation of pickets, ie where the pickets are changed from day to day to make it more difficult for an employer to identify them and for the courts to enforce an injunction against named individuals.

176. Such a procedure, it has been argued, would be analogous to Order 113 of the Rules of the Supreme Court which was introduced to deal with the problem of squatters. The Order provides a procedure for recovering possession of land or a building occupied by unknown persons. However, there are fundamental differences between this procedure and that proposed for proceeding against unnamed pickets. In the former case the procedure is for the repossession of private premises which belong to someone who is entitled to their recovery. In the case of picketing, which normally takes place outside the employer's premises on the highway or pavement there can be no question of recovering possession: everyone has a right of access to the highway. Again, once the Order 113 procedure has been used and the premises repossessed, there is usually no question of recurrence. In the case of picketing, however, the removal of one set of pickets might well be followed by the arrival of further pickets who in turn would need to be removed.

177. For such a procedure to be effective in the case of picketing, it would be necessary to make provision, on the application of the employer, for defined places to be made "no-go" areas for secondary pickets. They would then have to be kept clear by the police. Moreover, there would appear to be difficulties in applying this principle only to secondary pickets. To do so would mean the police having to distinguish between primary and secondary pickets and other people with legitimate business in the area. They are not readily in a position to do this. On the other hand, to stop everyone from entering a given area would mean creating areas where, if only temporarily, the right of passage along the highway and the right of free speech for the purposes of peacefully communicating and persuading no longer applied. Moreover, whatever the details of the proposal, it would again seem that the services of the police were being enlisted on behalf of the employer. There would also be practical difficulty in defining the geographical area to which any such procedure should apply, the length of time for which it should remain in force and who should be allowed to appear as defendant in any action, should a union or group of workers wish to contest it.

178. Abandoning the principle of the neutrality of the police could have serious implications. Without clear evidence that employers are being seriously frustrated from taking advantage of the provisions of the Employment Act 1980 by their inability to secure the names and addresses of pickets, it may in any case be thought premature at this time to consider making a change in the law of this nature.

Conclusion

179. The Government would welcome views on the issues considered in this Section.

D DEFINITION OF A TRADE DISPUTE

180. As the three previous Sections have shown, the immunities from actions in tort for individuals under Section 13 of the Trade Union and Labour Relations Act 1974 (as amended) apply only to acts done "in contemplation or furtherance of a trade dispute". If a dispute is not a trade dispute, as defined in legislation, then there is no immunity for the organisers of industrial action which arises from it.

181. This has led to suggestions that the definition of "trade dispute" itself should be changed. Since the definition applies to the immunity for industrial action generally, this would involve limitations on primary, as well as secondary, action. Some of the main proposals for change are considered below.

Development of the definition

182. The present definition of "trade dispute" is contained in Section 29 of the Trade Union and Labour Relations Act 1974. It has undergone considerable change in form, but only minor changes in substance, since it first appeared in legislation in the Trade Disputes Act 1906. Section 5(3) of that Act said that the expression "trade dispute" meant:

". . . any dispute between employers and workmen or, between workmen and workmen which is connected with the employment or non-employment, or the terms of employment, or with the conditions of labour, of any person, and the expression "workmen" means all persons employed in trade or industry, whether or not in the employment of the employer with whom a trade dispute arises".

183. In the Industrial Relations Act 1971, the 1906 definition was replaced by a new definition of "industrial dispute". This was more specific on the matters which were the legitimate subject of an industrial dispute than the original definition. But in general intention and effect the new definition was not very different from that of 1906.

46

184. There were, however, two more controversial changes:

(a) for a dispute to be an industrial dispute under the 1971 Act it had to "relate wholly or mainly" to one or more of the trade matters specified in the definition, whereas under the 1906 Act a trade dispute had only to be "connected with" those matters; and

(b) the 1971 definition did not include disputes between "workmen and workmen".

185. In Section 29 of the Trade Union and Labour Relations Act 1974 a new definition of "trade dispute" replaced the 1971 definition of "industrial dispute". The form used, however, was that of the 1971 rather than the 1906 Act. The main changes were:

(a) a reversal of the position on worker and worker disputes and on "wholly or mainly", described in the previous paragraph;

(b) several additions to the list of matters which could be the subject of a trade dispute to cover, in particular, disputes about membership and non-membership of a trade union and about recognition, both of which had been covered implicitly, but not explicitly, in the 1971 definition; and

(c) an extension of the definition to include disputes relating to matters outside Great Britain.

186. Despite these changes, most commentators have come to agree that, with the two exceptions noted in paragraph 184 above, the 1974 definition of "trade dispute" is not significantly different from its predecessors of 1971 and 1906. Nor has it been the focus of the same degree of discussion as other aspects of the immunities. Even so, there have been a number of cases since 1974 which have turned at least partly on the definition of "trade dispute" and raised questions about its scope. The three most interesting are:

• *BBC v Hearn* (1977), which involved the threat by BBC technicians to stop the transmission of the Cup Final to South Africa;

• *NWl. v Nelson & Woods* (1979), which concerned the attempt by the International Transport Workers' Federation (ITF) to black the ship "Nawala" when it delivered iron ore to the British Steel Corporation at Redcar; and

• *Express Newspapers v Keys and others* (1980), which concerned the threat by print unions to call out their members on the TUC's "day of action" against Government policy.

47

The implications of these cases are discussed below in the context of possible changes to the definition of trade dispute.

Possible changes in the definition

(i) Subject of a trade dispute

187. The subjects with which a trade dispute must be connected are now listed in Section 29(1) of the 1974 Act.[1] Though the list is more detailed than that contained in the 1906 definition and includes a number of items which were not specifically covered in the 1971 definition, it now seems to be generally accepted that a return to the more vaguely worded format of 1906 would create uncertainties about the scope of the definition without necessarily making it narrower. Nor have there been demands for any of the subjects listed in Section 29(1) to be removed.

188. Some criticism has, however, continued to focus on the requirement that a dispute need only be "connected with" one or more of the matters listed in the Section. This is particularly so following the House of Lords' judgement in the case of *NWL v Nelson and Woods*. In this case it was argued that the predominant purpose of the attempt to black the "Nawala" at Redcar was the furtherance of the ITF's world-wide campaign against "flags of convenience" shipping, and that it had little to do with the legitimate subjects of a trade dispute listed in the 1974 Act. In rejecting this argument, the House of Lords made it clear that as long as there was a genuine connection between the dispute and the subjects listed in the Act it did not matter that other issues were predominant. As Lord Scarman said in his judgement:

> "If the connection is only "ostensible", there is no connection. But predominance of subject matter is an irrelevance, provided always that there is a real connection between the dispute and one or other of the matters mentioned in the subsection. A dispute may be political or personal in character and yet be connected with, for example, the terms and conditions of employment of workers: such a dispute would be within the subsection. It is only if the alleged connection is a pretext or cover for another dispute which is in no way connected with any of the matters mentioned in the subsection that it is possible to hold that the dispute is not a trade dispute".

---

[1] The subjects listed in Section 29(1) are:
(a) terms and conditions of employment, or the physical conditions in which any workers are required to work;
(b) engagement or non-engagement, or termination or suspension of employment or the duties of employment, of one or more workers;
(c) allocation of work or the duties of employment as between workers or groups of workers;
(d) matters of discipline;
(e) the membership or non-membership of a trade union on the part of a worker;
(f) facilities for officials of trade unions; and
(g) machinery for negotiation or consultation, and other procedures, relating to any of the foregoing matters, including the recognition by employers or employers' associations of the right of a trade union to represent workers in any such negotiation or consultation or in the carrying out of such procedures.

189. It is argued that this is entirely unacceptable and that it extends the definition of trade dispute in a new and unexpected way.[1] As a result, it is claimed, trade union officials have virtually complete freedom to pursue disputes of a purely personal and political character and to call strikes which have only the slightest connection with the subjects of a trade dispute.

190. It has been argued that there should be some measurement of the importance of the trade dispute element and that a dispute should only fall within the definition of trade dispute if that element is found to be significant compared with other elements. Various methods of achieving this are proposed. One way would be to return to the 1971 position where the dispute had to be related "wholly or mainly to" one or more of the matters listed in the Act. Another possibility would be to require that one or more of the subjects listed should be predominant or that it be a substantial or significant element in the dispute.

191. The main argument against this approach is that in many disputes it is by no means easy to separate the different elements or to decide which is predominant, and that it would put the courts in an invidious position to require them to do so. The judgement in the "Nawala" case itself shows that in the dispute questions about the terms and conditions of the ship's crew and of seamen worldwide were inextricably bound up with the ITF's campaign against flags of convenience. Even if the courts had decided it was valid to apply a test of predominant purpose it would have been by no means easy to establish which motive was predominant.

(ii) Political disputes

192. This question of mixed motives is also relevant to the position of the political dispute or strike. The term "political" has been associated with many different types of disputes over the years. It would probably be generally agreed that political strikes normally involve persuading the Government to change its policies. But there would be much less agreement on when, in any particular instance, a strike should be described as "political". As Lord Justice Roskill said in the case of *Sherard v AUEW* in 1973:

"Although the phrase 'political strike' has from time to time been used in reported cases, it is to my mind a phrase which should be used, at any rate in a court of law, with considerable caution, for it does not readily lend itself to precise or accurate definition. It is all too easy for someone to talk of a strike as being a 'political strike' when what that person really means is that the object of the strike is something of which he as an individual subjectively disapproves".

[1] It is possible, for example, that the House of Lords' decision in the "Nawala" case has cast doubt on the decision of the House of Lords in the case of *Conway v Wade* in 1909 that a case of a personal grudge between a union official and a union member was not a trade dispute.

193. The present law is silent on the distinction between a political dispute and a trade dispute. As has been seen, a dispute is a trade dispute if it satisfies the definition in Section 29 of the Trade Union and Labour Relations Act 1974, whether or not it also includes a political element. This means in effect that a political dispute will be outside the definition of trade dispute where:

(a) the parties to the dispute are not, respectively, employers and workers or workers and workers—eg where there is a dispute between workers and the Government (when the Government is not their employer);

(b) the dispute is not connected with any of the subject matters listed.

194. There are two recent examples of political disputes where the courts have decided that the dispute did not come within the definition of trade dispute in Section 29. In *BBC v Hearn* in 1977 the Court of Appeal granted an injunction against the General Secretary and Executive Council Members of the Association of Broadcasting Staffs to restrain the threatened blacking of the BBC's transmission via satellite of the Cup Final to South Africa. The Court decided that the subject of the dispute—the union's support for a campaign against the policies of the South African Government—was not within the definition of trade dispute in Section 29 and that, therefore, the organisers of the threatened action had no immunity.

195. The second case concerned the TUC's "day of action" on 14 May 1980 against the Government's policies. Express Newspapers Ltd and the Evening Standard sought an injunction against the General Secretaries of the main printing unions and of the NUJ to restrain them from calling their members out on strike on that day. Mr Justice Griffiths found that the action was taken against the Government to protest at the Government's policies:

"... there was no trade dispute in the present case. It was an avowed political strike and none of the unions concerned had averred that they were entitled to immunity under Section 13".

196. It is clear from these cases that a purely political strike which has no connection with the subjects listed in Section 29 falls outside the definition of trade dispute and has no immunity. But, as has been seen, under the present law, as long as there is a genuine connection with the subject matters listed in Section 29, then a dispute, however political it may seem, comes within the statutory definition of a trade dispute.

197. It is sometimes argued that the current law allows far too much scope for trade unions to call strikes which are designed simply to express opposition to public policies or to put pressure on the Government to change them. On this view a change in the law is overdue.

198. Two possible changes are put forward most frequently. First there is the approach, discussed in paragraphs 190 and 191 above, which would require a legitimate trade dispute to be "wholly or mainly" related to the

subjects listed in Section 29. How this would affect political strikes would depend to a large extent on the courts' interpretation of the statute. As has been seen, in many cases it would be very difficult indeed to sort out the different elements of a dispute and decide which element was predominant. This is likely to be particularly so in the case of a public sector dispute where the Government is the direct employer or a main provider of finance and where arguments about terms and conditions of employment can be inextricably tied up with attempts to persuade the Government to change its policy.

199. The second, and more radical, approach would be to remove immunity from disputes with a political element. The difficulty, however, would be in finding a generally acceptable definition of "political". Furthermore, such an approach would remove immunity from a wide range of industrial action in what would otherwise be regarded as perfectly legitimate disputes about terms and conditions of employment where Government is either the employer or the provider of money to the employer.

200. A major difficulty with either of these proposals is that they would narrow the definition in a way which would inevitably restrict many types of industrial action which are undoubtedly directed at improving terms and conditions of employment. It is argued that the current definition of trade dispute strikes the right balance between outlawing the purely political strike and recognising that disputes which are partly about terms and conditions can well have a political element. As proponents of this view point out, despite occasional attempts to deal with political strikes, the present position has survived without major difficulty since 1906.

(iii) Parties to the dispute

201. Another area in which there has been criticism of the trade dispute definition is in relation to the parties to a trade dispute allowed by Section 29. Under this Section a trade dispute may be a dispute between employers and workers or workers and workers; and for the purpose of this Section "employers" includes employers' associations and "workers" covers trade unions.

202. There have been two main criticisms:

(a) that the definition should not include "worker and worker" disputes which do not involve an employer;

(b) that the present definition allows trade unions to be in dispute with an employer when none of that employer's employees are in dispute with him.

These are considered in turn below.

(a) Worker and worker disputes

203. The definition of a trade dispute in the 1906 Act included disputes between workers. The justification for this has been questioned, especially as such disputes usually include the employer. In fact, the legal position of disputes between workers and workers has been changed by Section

51

17 of the Employment Act. As a result of this Section, primary action can only be organised lawfully when it is to be taken by employees of an employer who is party to a trade dispute; action by employees of an employer not in dispute is by definition secondary action which in order to be organised lawfully must meet the conditions set out in Section 17. The effect of this is that industrial action in a worker and worker dispute which interferes with commercial contracts will have no immunity unless it involves an employer who is party to the dispute.

204. It remains to be seen how far this restricts industrial action in worker and worker disputes. The Government's view, as explained in the debates on the Employment Bill, is that it is unlikely to make much difference since, in most cases, disputes between workers or trade unions automatically involve the employer of the workers concerned. To take an example, one group of workers may be in dispute over its desire to maintain pay differentials over another group. However, both groups are likely to be able to claim successfully that they are also in dispute with their employer over a pay demand, although the dispute clearly arises from a disagreement between workers. The case of *Cory Lighterage Ltd v TGWU* in 1973 raised the possibility, however, that some demarcation disputes and disputes between unions as to union membership might fall into the category of "pure" worker and worker disputes with no employer involvement. But even in that case the Court of Appeal commented on how easily such disputes could grow to involve the employer.

205. It may be that the only question which remains, therefore, is whether, as a result of the Employment Act, the reference to disputes between workers and workers in Section 29 of the Trade Union and Labour Relations Act 1974 is necessary. It is arguable that the Act has made the reference redundant.

(b) *Trade unions as parties to the dispute*

206. There has also been criticism of the fact that there can be a trade dispute (as defined in Section 29) between a trade union and an employer, even though none of the employer's employees are involved in the dispute. This arises partly because under Section 29(4) a trade union can be a party to a trade dispute in its own right and partly because under Section 29(6) workers who are party to a dispute need not be employed by the employer with whom they are in dispute.

207. Attention was focused on this question by the facts of *NWL v Nelson and Woods* (the "Nawala" case) which has been referred to above. It appeared that the attempts by the ITF to organise blacking of the "Nawala" at Redcar were not supported by the ship's largely Hong Kong crew. Indeed, the owners of the "Nawala" at one point produced sworn statements by crew members that they did not support the union's action and were unwilling to sign the ITF's standard agreement on terms and conditions.

208. The question is how far is it justified for a trade union to be in dispute with an employer whose employees are entirely content with their

terms and conditions? Is there not a right for employees to work undisturbed on terms of employment that they find acceptable and to have the protection of the law if anyone tries to stop them? Those who believe it is not justified argue for changes to the definition of "trade dispute" which would either (or both):

(a) reverse the effects of Section 29(6) so that for there to be a trade dispute between an employer and workers it would be necessary for some of those workers to be employed by that employer; and/or

(b) mean that a trade union could only be a party to a trade dispute if some of the employees in dispute were members of the trade union or wanted to join.

209. Two main arguments are to be found against such a proposal. First, it is said that a trade union has a responsibility to all its members, not just to the employees in a particular firm. It is held that this justifies the organisation of action against a company when the union considers the interests of its members to be under threat, even if it has no members in that company. The second argument is that to make the existence of a trade dispute dependent on trade union members working for the employer in dispute would give positive encouragement to the employer who sought to prevent union organisation developing in his firm by sacking anyone who joined the union. On this view it is argued that, as long as the employer is successful in preventing union members being employed in his firm, the union would be unjustifiably deprived of any legitimate redress against him.

(iv) International shipping

210. It has also been suggested that special provision should be made on the lines of the proposal in paragraph 208(a) to prevent the blacking of international shipping in British ports when there is and has been no dispute involving the crews of those ships past or present. This proposal arises from the international shipping community's view that the House of Lords' judgement in the "Nawala" case has left foreign ships coming to Great Britain particularly vulnerable to the campaign by the ITF against the use of "flags of convenience". This involves attempts by the ITF to get its constituent trade unions in ports throughout the Western world to black what they hold to be "flags of convenience" shipping even where a ship has always sailed under a "flag of convenience" and there is no question of one crew having been replaced by another paid at lower rates.

211. The arguments for and against such a change go much wider than domestic industrial relations policies. In favour of a change, it is argued that it is wrong in principle to apply British law, based on an evaluation of domestic industrial relations, to foreign ships with different industrial relations problems and which are outside the jurisdiction of British law as soon as they sail out of territorial waters. It is also said that our legislation makes it much easier to pursue a campaign of blacking in British ports than in any other Western European ports. As a result, it is argued first, that Britain's international trade and commerce will suffer because only high-cost shipping will be prepared to risk coming to our ports, and that this could put at hazard jobs in Britain which depend on international trade.

53

Secondly, it is argued that British shipping will be exposed to similiar treatment in foreign ports; and that this will put at risk British seafarers' jobs, which are heavily dependent on the preservation of the freedom of the seas.

212. Against these considerations the ITF claims that it has a responsibility to all its constituent members: to Western European crews who fear that "flags of convenience" ships may be used in some cases to undercut their wages or to threaten their jobs; and to crews from the Third World who, the Federation believes, are particularly vulnerable to exploitation by employers. (It must be observed that not all ITF affiliates support the ITF's action). The ITF would argue that the transient nature of the link between workers and any particular employer in international shipping means that seamen are always in an inherently weaker position *vis a vis* their employer, and that the balance can only be restored, and then only partially, by industrial action taken at ports where ships flying "flags of convenience" call. Lord Denning said in his judgement in the "Nawala" case:

> "The only weapon . . . at the disposal of the ITF (which they can use in order to ensure fair play for seamen and the like) is the weapon of 'blacking'. If it were taken away in this case it would mean that it would be taken away virtually in all the cases in which they operate for the benefit of seafaring men".

213. The question is whether the operation of the present definition of trade dispute is satisfactory in relation to international shipping for the reasons set out in paragraphs 210–211 above and whether consideration should be given to making such changes in the law as are needed to protect ships in British ports from industrial action in cases where there is and has been no dispute to which members of the crew are a party. It would of course be necessary to continue to allow lawful industrial action to be taken in furtherance of disputes concerning the dismissal of any members of the crews.

Conclusion

214. The Government would welcome views on the issues discussed in paragraphs 210–213 and the others considered in this Section and particularly on the following questions:

(a) have problems arisen in areas other than those mentioned due to the current definition of "trade dispute"?

(b) are changes needed in the areas discussed in this Section or in other areas?

(c) what is likely to be the practical effect of any changes on the immunity for industrial action?

E. LEGALLY ENFORCEABLE COLLECTIVE AGREEMENTS

215. A distinguishing feature of British industrial relations is the absence of legally enforceable collective agreements. In most Western industrial countries collective agreements are contracts which are enforceable by and

against those who are parties to them. This imposes upon those parties a "peace", or "no strike, no lock-out" obligation which makes it unlawful to use industrial action to try to change the provisions of an agreement while it is in force.

216. Two main advantages are claimed for legally enforceable collective agreements. First, it is argued that they bring a period of peace and stability to industrial relations in a company or industry which benefits both employers and employees. From the employer's point of view, he can plan his business for the period ahead on the basis of clearly predictable labour costs and in the knowledge that production is unlikely to be interrupted by industrial action. In turn, employees are likely to benefit in terms of higher wages and greater job security from the higher productivity which a strike-free period makes possible.

217. Legally enforceable collective agreements do not necessarily mean that fewer days are lost because of strikes, but strikes tend to be concentrated in the period of renegotiation of the agreement. The USA is cited as an example. The Americans have lost about the same number of days per person through strikes as Great Britain in recent years, but 90 per cent of these strikes have been concentrated in the period of renegotiation. This is a major advantage and enables managers to turn their minds to running an efficient business and creating wealth, rather than be diverted by or absorbed in problems of industrial relations as often happens in this country.

218. A second advantage, it is argued, is that legally enforceable collective agreements foster a more professional approach to bargaining on the part of both employers and unions. The agreements reached are likely to be more comprehensive as to the rights and obligations of the parties and less likely to contain uncertainties or ambiguities which may provide grounds for disputes. In particular, it is suggested that they encourage the development of more sophisticated disputes procedures to resolve any issues which might arise on the interpretation or application of agreements, and a greater willingness to use such procedures to resolve disputes.

219. The question considered here is whether legally enforceable collective agreements could be developed in Great Britain and, if they were, whether some or all of these advantages could be expected. A particular defect of industrial relations in this country in recent years has been too great a readiness to resort to strikes regardless of the currency of a collective agreement and before the procedures for resolving disputes have been exhausted. The resultant spasmodic disruption to production and the provision of services has been very costly and has resulted in industry failing to meet delivery dates with a consequent loss of orders and markets. Industry and the community generally would benefit enormously if the advantages which legally enforceable agreements appear to have brought to other countries could be realised here.

220. It is suggested that industrial action should not have immunity where it is taken in breach of a collective agreement. This could apply either to action which was taken during the currency of the collective agreement itself, or if it were desired to concentrate on the development and use of disputes procedures, to action which was taken before the agreed procedure for resolving disputes had been exhausted. Its effect would be to enable an employer damaged by a strike or other industrial action in breach of an agreement to sue the organisers of the action for an injunction or damages.

221. Removing immunity from industrial action in breach of an agreement would not in fact make the agreements themselves legally binding contracts, as they are in most other countries though the effects would be similar. This is because removal of immunity in this way affects only the *organisers* of industrial action which breaks an agreement. It would not necessarily bind the parties to the agreement to honour its other provisions.

222. In other countries the effect of legally enforceable agreements is not only to impose a peace obligation which restricts the power to organise industrial action. It also places corresponding obligations on the employer who is party to the agreement to observe its terms by maintaining the wages and conditions which have been agreed. The Donovan Commission commented:

"Legislation giving contractual force to collective agreements may conceivably be passed without any corresponding step being taken towards giving to the terms and conditions laid down in agreements the force of a compulsory code. But, whilst conceivable, such legislation would in its character and impact on industrial relations be different from legal systems in which the obligation to keep the peace is intertwined and co-extensive with the compulsion to apply the terms of the agreement. It is because and in so far as the law guarantees those terms that the unions are made to guarantee the peace. To enact the peace obligation as a legal obligation without the corresponding legal guarantee for the enforcement of the substantive terms of the agreement would be an unusual step in labour legislation which only very exceptional circumstances could justify." (paragraph 469)

223. If, therefore, it were decided to remove immunity from industrial action which was in breach of a collective agreement, it would seem necessary to consider also whether collective agreements should be made legally enforceable contracts binding equally on the parties to them.

Legally enforceable agreements in Great Britain

224. It has been noted that, unlike most other countries, Great Britain has no tradition of legally enforceable agreements. They are not prohibited

by law. But management and unions have chosen not to conclude agreements which are legally binding. The Donovan Commission summed up the position as follows:

> "In this country collective agreements are not legally binding contracts. This is not because the law says that they are not contracts or that the parties to them may not give them the force of contracts . . . It is due to the intention of the parties themselves. They do not intend to make a legally binding contract, and without both parties intending to be legally bound there can be no contract in the legal sense . . . this intention and policy that collective bargaining and collective agreements should remain outside the law, is one of the characteristic features of our system of industrial relations . . . It is deeply rooted in its structure." (paragraphs 470–471)

225. The High Court confirmed that collective agreements were not legally binding in 1969 in the case of *Ford Motor Co v Amalgamated Union of Engineering and Foundry Workers (AEF)*. Mr Justice Geoffrey Lane (the present Lord Chief Justice) giving judgement said:

> "The fact that the agreements *prima facie* deal with commercial relationships is outweighed by the other considerations, by the wording of the agreements, by the nature of the agreements, and by the climate of opinion voiced and evidenced by the extra-judicial authorities . . . Without clear and express provisions making them amenable to legal action, they remain in the realm of undertakings binding in honour".

226. There is a history of proposals to encourage the development of legally enforceable agreements by statute. The White Paper "In Place of Strife" published in 1969 proposed a power for the Secretary of State for Employment to order a return to work for 28 days if a strike occurred in breach of a procedure agreement and to require a compulsory ballot of the workforce. This proposal was strongly opposed by the trade unions.

227. More important, the Industrial Relations Act 1971 made collective agreements, including procedure agreements, legally binding unless they included a specific provision to the contrary. It thus became an unfair industrial practice for any party to break a legally enforceable agreement or for a trade union or employers' association not to take all reasonable steps to prevent its members from breaking an agreement. Where there was no procedure agreement in force, or there was industrial action in breach of an existing agreement, the Secretary of State for Employment (or in some circumstances a party to an agreement) could seek from the NIRC a reference to the Commission on Industrial Relations, which could then recommend that new or revised procedures should be adopted. Such recommendations were legally enforceable if, after 6 months, the parties concerned failed to reach agreement themselves.

228. The Act, however, did not result in any increase in legally enforceable agreements. Indeed, virtually every agreement concluded after the Act became law included a provision that the agreement was not to be regarded

as legally enforceable (a provision which is still included in some agreements) and the power for the Secretary of State to make references to the Commission for Industrial Relations was never used.

229. When the Industrial Relations Act was repealed in 1974 the legal presumption was reversed. Following the Trade Union and Labour Relations Act 1974 collective agreements are *not* enforceable at law unless the parties to the agreement agree otherwise.

230. The present position, therefore, is as the Donovan Commission described it in 1968. The lack of legally binding collective agreements remains one of the features of British industrial relations which sets it most clearly apart from its counterparts in Western Europe and the USA.

Main considerations

231. Against this background how successfully could legally enforceable collective agreements be introduced into this country? There are three main considerations.

(i) The informal system of collective bargaining

232. The first is how to reconcile legally enforceable agreements with the system of collective bargaining which has developed in Great Britain. A system of legal enforceability requires collective agreements to be clear, precise and capable of interpretation in the courts in disputed cases. The vast majority of collective agreements in this country are vague, imprecise and underpinned by informal understandings based on long standing custom and practice.

233. The Donovan Commission drew attention to this problem in its report. It said:

" . . . collective bargaining takes place at a number of levels simultaneously, and, in so far as it takes place at workshop or plant level, it is fragmented and it is informal. That it is fragmented means, from the legal point of view, that it is difficult and perhaps often impossible to identify the 'party' who made it on the workers' side, and that it is informal means that it would sometimes and probably very often be impossible for a court to receive evidence enabling it to ascertain the content of the 'agreement' in a way required for its legal enforcement. In fact most of these 'agreements' would probably, in the legal sense, be 'void for uncertainty'. Industry-wide bargaining and workshop or plant bargaining are however closely intertwined. To enforce one without the other would be to distort the effect of our collective bargaining system. That system is today a patchwork of formal agreements, informal agreements and 'custom and practice'. No court, asked to 'enforce' a collective agreement, could disentangle the 'agreement' from the inarticulate practices which are its background." (paragraph 472)

A year after the Commission reported, its view was confirmed by the High Court in the Ford Motor Co case to which reference has already been made. In his judgement Mr Justice Geoffrey Lane described collective agreements in this country as "composed largely of optimistic aspirations, presenting grave practical problems of enforcement . . ."

234. It is arguable that any attempt to impose the legal enforceability of collective agreements by law would be unsuccessful without changes to the nature of collective bargaining. This was very much the conclusion the Donovan Commission reached on the issue. It concluded that a final decision on legally enforceable agreements should be deferred until its recommendations for reforming collective bargaining had been followed. It is not possible to hold that these looked for reforms have yet been generally adopted.

235. An alternative view was reflected in the provisions of the Industrial Relations Act 1971. In addition to making collective agreements legally enforceable (with provision for contracting out), the Act set up detailed procedures under which both the Secretary of State and the Commission on Industrial Relations had responsibility for developing procedure agreements in those industries where they did not already exist or had been shown to be inadequate. The aim was to encourage changes in the collective bargaining system which, it was hoped, would make legal enforceability effective. As has been noted above, however, this procedure was not invoked during the lifetime of the Act.

(ii) Liability of trade unions

236. In some other countries the legal enforceability of collective agreements means that trade unions themselves become liable if their officials or members break those agreements. It can readily be argued that, in principle, if a union official has entered into an agreement involving his members in a particular company, the union should have responsibility for seeking to ensure that the agreement is observed. That was the principle on which the Industrial Relations Act 1971 made it an unfair industrial practice for a trade union "not to take all such steps as are reasonably practicable" to prevent its members from acting in breach of undertakings in a collective agreement.

237. The general question of the vicarious liability of trade unions for the unlawful acts of their officials and members is discussed elsewhere (see paragraphs 116–122). But, in addition, it is argued that trade unions are not at present equipped to supervise and monitor the multiplicity of agreements which are signed by their officials, including shop stewards. Without major changes in the structure and organisation of unions (including a substantial increase in the number of full-time officials), it is suggested that it would be unrealistic to expect them to exercise the necessary degree of control over the making of such agreements which is apparent in other countries. To legislate to make them responsible could, in the absence of such changes, compound the problems of applying the concept of vicarious

responsibility to trade unions. However, against this it can be argued that those problems are exaggerated and that unions should, and could, be expected to adapt to new legal responsibilities with consequent benefits for the conduct of industrial relations.

238. These considerations apply also—although perhaps to a lesser extent—in relation to employers' associations and employers. In particular, it would be necessary to establish how far an employers' association was to be held responsible for the enforcement of an industry-wide agreement, including a procedure agreement, against individual employers.

(iii) Attitudes of employers and trade unions

239. The third consideration lies in the attitudes of employers and unions. If both employers and trade union negotiators had accepted that it was in their interests to conclude legally binding agreements they could have done so at any time in the last 100 years. They have hardly ever done so. The 1971 Act sought to encourage the adoption of such agreements. The experience was that management and unions were at best apathetic and at worst deeply hostile. Hostility appears to have been greater on the part of unions, reflecting their traditional suspicion of legal intervention in collective bargaining, but it is by no means clear that employers would always have welcomed the stricter obligations legal enforceability would impose on them. The informal nature of collective bargaining in Great Britain has often appeared to suit both employers and trade unions, although to different extents at different times.

240. It is argued that there needs to be some general basis of consent for the universal introduction of legally enforceable agreements into Great Britain for the system to operate effectively. The experience of other countries shows that legal enforceability works, not simply because the law provides that agreements are enforceable at law, but because it is accepted by both unions and management alike as a sensible way of regulating industrial relations which benefits employers and their employees.

241. Our own experience suggests that legislation alone might be unlikely to bring about the necessary change in attitudes. If the legislation allowed the parties to collective agreements to opt out of legal enforceability (for example, by an express provision in an agreement that a person is not to be subject to legal action if he acts in breach of it) as is the case with contracts generally, the experience of the 1971 Act suggests that everyone might do so. On the other hand, to impose a compulsory system of enforceability would be to reverse the long established principle of law that the parties can decide whether or not to make contracts legally enforceable. It could be evaded by those who were determined to do so. Trade unions in particular might well seek to avoid legal enforceability by the simple expedient of refusing to conclude new written agreements at all and by withdrawing from existing procedure agreements. If so, the effect would be the reverse of that intended.

Conclusion

242. The experience of other countries suggests there could be advantages in introducing legally enforceable collective agreements in Great Britain. For employers they could undoubtedly provide a period of stable industrial relations and continuous production which is a prerequisite for efficient and expanding business and the planning of investment. If these benefits were realised the consequent benefits for trade unions and their members would be appreciable: higher wages, improved conditions and greater job security in return for guarantees of industrial peace. It can be argued that present bargaining practices in Great Britain ought to be changed and legal enforceability of collective agreements could be an important lever to secure such change.

243. It might be, however, that given the history and practice of industrial relations in Great Britain, the task of convincing negotiators of the value of legal enforceability is primarily an educational one and an essential prerequisite is still the need to secure an improvement in the nature of collective bargaining and the form of agreements concluded, particularly procedure agreements. A very significant change in practice would seem to be necessary to avoid the difficulties the courts would otherwise have in establishing what were the provisions and intentions of existing agreements. Without such changes, and without an established basis of consent, it is possible that any attempt to impose legally enforceable collective agreements would be hindered by evasion of the kind described in paragraph 241 and by the difficulty the courts would face.

244. The Government would welcome views:

(i) on this analysis of the advantages and difficulties of changing the law to remove immunities from industrial action taken in breach of collective agreements and of securing the widespread application of enforceable agreements in this country;

(ii) in the light of the advantages of introducing legally enforceable agreements in Great Britain, on the steps which might be taken to encourage progress towards this.

F SECRET BALLOTS

245. The practice of holding secret ballots for the election of union officers or to decide whether or not to accept a specific pay offer or to take industrial action is well established in some trade unions. But this practice is still very far from being general and progress in extending it has been slow. The importance of proper democratic procedures for the election—and periodic re-election—of union officials is pointed out in paragraph 20. Only the adoption of such procedures will enable trade unions to meet the criticism that their leaders are often out of touch with the views of their members and sometimes pursue policies which the majority of their members do not support. The Government has accordingly taken

steps through the Employment Act 1980 to provide funds for the use of secret ballots in trade union elections and for other purposes (see paragraph 251 below).

246. This Section is concerned with the specific issue of secret ballots before industrial action is taken. The increasing damage industrial action can inflict on the community has led to demands that the decision of a trade union to take such action should be reached only after fully consulting the wishes of its members. Too often in recent years it has seemed that employees have been called out on strike by their unions without proper consultation and sometimes against their express wishes. In many cases it has appeared that employees have had no choice but to obey the union instruction or to face the threat of expulsion from the union. This has led to increasing demands for trade unions to hold secret ballots before a strike is called. A number of proposals have been advanced to ensure that industrial action is called by a trade union only when it demonstrably has the support of the union members concerned in a secret ballot. In particular, it has been proposed that immunity for calling industrial action should be made dependent in certain circumstances on the union having had a ballot of the members to determine whether the majority wish that industrial action to be taken. Some have gone further and urged that immunities should only be available for those trade unions which adopt democratic procedures for both elections and strike decisions.

247. Proposals for making secret ballots before industrial action mandatory are not new. The Donovan Commission, for example, examined and rejected a proposal that an affirmative secret ballot should be held if the organisers of a strike were to have immunity. They pointed out that such a proposal could apply only to major official strikes: it would clearly be impracticable for it to apply to industrial action of every type, however brief and spontaneous. They concluded that there was little justification for the view that workers were less likely to vote for strike action than their leaders. Experience in the USA and in Canada had been that strike ballots were likely to go in favour of strike action. The Commission saw other objections to making such ballots compulsory. Once a strike began after it had been endorsed by a ballot, an eventual settlement might be delayed by the restriction placed on union leaders' freedom of action. Moreover, how was the question on which the vote was to be taken to be framed? If the vote was, for instance, about whether to accept the employer's latest offer, what was to happen if the employer subsequently made a slightly improved offer?

248. Another proposal, that the Secretary of State should be able to require a union to hold a secret ballot before a major official strike, was considered in 1969 in the Labour Government's White Paper, "In Place of Strife". The White Paper said that it was "a matter for concern that at present it is possible for a major official strike to be called when the support of those involved may be in doubt". It proposed that the Secretary of State should have discretionary power to require the union or unions involved to hold a ballot on the question of strike action. The power would

62

be used where the Secretary of State believed that the proposed strike would "involve a serious threat to the economy or public interest" and there was doubt whether it commanded the support of those concerned.

249. A similar provision was included in the Industrial Relations Act 1971. Under Section 141 of the Act the Secretary of State could, in a major dispute which threatened the national interest, apply to the NIRC for an order requiring a ballot where industrial action had begun or was threatened and where he considered that there were doubts whether the workers concerned supported the industrial action or had had the opportunity of expressing their views.[1]

250. Only one ballot, which was by post, was in fact conducted. It covered 175,000 British Rail employees and was held in May 1972, following an application by the Secretary of State for Employment to the NIRC, to discover whether, in the light of British Rail's pay offer, its employees were in favour of further industrial action. 85 per cent of those entitled to vote did so and votes in favour amounted to 129,441 votes against to 23,181 with 1,567 abstentions.[2]

Effects of the Employment Act 1980

251. The Employment Act 1980 encourages greater use of secret ballots in a number of ways. Section 1 makes funds available to trade unions, through the Certification Officer, towards the cost of postal ballots. Section 2 requires employers to make available premises for the holding of workplace ballots. The Code of Practice on Closed Shop Agreements and Arrangements[3], which must be taken into account where relevant in cases before industrial tribunals, says (paragraph 54) that disciplinary action or the threat of it should not be taken against a member whose only "offence" is that he refused to take part in industrial action called for by his union on the ground that the action had not been affirmed in a secret ballot. The aim of these provisions is to encourage union members to seek secret strike ballots and unions to hold them. Those in the union movement who oppose such decision-making in industrial disputes and elections are deprived of their most credible argument against secret ballots—the "prohibitive" cost. There is a heavier onus on them to explain to the membership as a whole why they opposed secret ballots and why individual members should be denied the opportunity of registering their views in secret.

252. It has been argued that the law should go further. Several related proposals for making immunity dependent on the holding of secret ballots were debated during the passage of the Employment Bill. Each embodied the principle that a proportion of a union's members involved in industrial

[1] For a discussion of the circumstances in which it applied see paragraphs 314-316.
[2] American experience also suggests that ballots of trade union members tend to support industrial action when called by union leaders (see paragraphs 317-319).
[3] The Code was issued by the Secretary of State for Employment under Section 3 of the Employment Act 1980 and became effective on 17 December 1980.

action should have the right to call for a secret ballot before or during that action. One proposal was that 500 members of the union or 15 per cent, whichever was the lower figure, should be able to require such a ballot. Once a valid request for a ballot had been made, immunities under Section 13 and/or Section 14 of the Trade Union and Labour Relations Act 1974 were to be withdrawn from any industrial action until a secret ballot had been held and the result had proved affirmative. Under a variant of this proposal, immunity would have been restored once a ballot had been held whatever its outcome, the purpose being to secure a ballot rather than to impose the views expressed through the ballot on the unions' decision-making bodies. In this way conflict with the unions' present arrangements might be avoided.

Main approaches to promoting secret ballots

253. It seems, therefore, that there are now two general approaches on how to promote ballots before strike action:

(i) proposals referred to in the previous paragraph for ballots "triggered" by union members; and

(ii) a belief that ballots can best be encouraged in a non-mandatory way, for example, by the provision of public funds.

The objectives of, and basic beliefs underlying, each approach are very similar. The proponents of both strongly support the wider use of secret ballots. They share a strong belief that, in a matter of such importance to an employee's livelihood as a strike, it is right that he should have the opportunity of registering his view on the issue in a secret ballot.

254. Furthermore, it is argued that several incidents in recent years have shown that national trade union leaders are out of touch with the views of rank and file members and have sought to call strikes against their wishes. Factory gate meetings or poorly attended branch meetings are a highly unsatisfactory means of taking decisions on matters as important as strikes.

255. The differences between the two approaches are those of means, emphasis and practicability. Those in favour of "triggered" ballots argue that the ballot should be the basis of decision-making in trade unions, just as it is an integral part of political democracy. It is suggested, moreover, that it is unreasonable to expect a significant extension of secret ballots by voluntary means when the existing holders of power in unions tend to see their use as a threat to their position. On this view, only action by Government can break their entrenched opposition. Therefore, it is suggested, the right of trade union members to participate in the decision-making process on a proposal to strike or to take another form of industrial action should be established in the law.

256. It is also argued that, just as Parliament has given shareholders in certain circumstances the right to call an extraordinary meeting of a limited company, so it should give trade unionists the right to call a ballot.

A distinction is drawn between ballots of this kind and the two forms of compulsory ballots discussed in paragraphs 247-250 above. Because the compulsion to hold the ballot is not being applied directly by the law or by the Secretary of State, but by the unions' own membership, it is argued that the proposals would be much more acceptable to the trade union movement.

257. As for the non-mandatory approach to ballots, its proponents argue that this is the better means of providing durable and effective encouragement to union ballots of all kinds. It is argued that the Government should not go beyond measures of the kind it has taken in the Employment Act 1980 which are intended to operate with the grain of responsible trade union leadership and to strengthen such leadership, not to undermine it.

258. Those who favour this approach argue that any imposition of requirements on unions to hold ballots could inhibit the greater use of secret ballots as normal union practice. It could be claimed by unions that the Government was seeking to interfere in their internal affairs, overriding their constitutions and rules which are themselves democratically determined. It is arguable that it would, therefore, be more difficult for responsible union leaders, who may wish to use the funds available under Section 1 of the Employment Act 1980, to do so.

259. It is further argued that there would be practical problems with any proposal for ballots "triggered" by union members. For example, how would it be determined whether the threshold required had been achieved? Where there was uncertainty (eg about the extent of the electorate, or whether a sufficient number of members were calling for a ballot), who would decide whether a ballot should be conducted and how long would this take? In the meantime, will there be immunity for industrial action or not? There could also be difficulties where several unions are involved. It might be necessary to involve some outside supervisory agency to take decisions on such questions but, if such a body were involved, the expected advantage of this approach—that it did not intervene in the affairs of the trade union—would be lost.

260. But perhaps the greatest problem posed by "triggered" ballots is whether they should apply to unofficial industrial action. If a compulsory ballot provision did not apply to unofficial action, which already constitutes the overwhelming majority of industrial action, such action would continue to enjoy immunity in which case a premium would be placed on irresponsible behaviour. On the other hand, if a compulsory ballot provision applied equally to unofficial action, it might be possible for unofficial strike leaders to use the ballot procedure to secure respectability and recognition.

Conclusion

261. This Section has discussed a variety of ways in which secret ballots before industrial action is taken might be encouraged or required. There

65

are differing views not on the objective but on the practicability of achieving it. The Government would welcome views on the practicalities and balance of advantage of making secret ballots compulsory and on what further steps might be taken to encourage their voluntary use.

G CLOSED SHOP AND UNION MEMBERSHIP ISSUES

262. The closed shop is the term customarily applied to an agreement or arrangement which requires employees to join a specified union as a condition of getting or holding a job.

263. The Government's view of the closed shop is clear: it is opposed to the principles underlying it. That people should be required to join a union as a condition of getting or holding a job runs contrary to the general traditions of personal liberty in this country. It is acceptable for a union to seek to increase its membership by voluntary means. What is objectionable, however, is to enforce membership by means of a closed shop as a condition of employment. Individual employees should have the right to decide for themselves whether or not to join a trade union. Closed shops and the practices they can engender damage the image of trade unionism itself. The Government believes that these views are increasingly shared, not least within trade unions themselves.

264. Closed shops are a major feature of British industry, covering about 5 million manual and white-collar workers, and they are found over a wide spectrum of industries in both the private and public sectors. There are many employers as well as trade unionists who hold that they are of importance in helping to create stability in industrial relations. It is argued that the closed shop helps to establish unions as stable and effective organisations representing the workforce as a whole; encourages the responsible cooperation of unions with each other and with management; and helps to ensure that unions have the ability to comply with, and see that their members comply with, agreements they enter into.

265. However, there is little evidence that closed shops have helped to reduce industrial conflict and some closed shops are undoubtedly used as a basis for establishing and maintaining restrictive practices which impede efficiency. The closed shop has been used increasingly as a means of denying business to, and in some cases threatening with extinction, firms whose employees are not members of a union. In some industries it has become common practice for union members working in a closed shop or in a firm where there is a high degree of union membership to refuse to handle goods from non-union sources or to let non-union employees of other companies work alongside them at the same place of work. The purpose of such action may be to compel the employees in non-union firms to become union members or to defend the jobs of union members against what is seen by the unions as a threat from non-union firms. It is arguable, however, that these practices are often more a means of protecting outdated and inefficient methods of working than of defending union members against

any more direct threat to their employment. In many other countries (including most of our more successful international competitors) the law declares the closed shop illegal or provides employees with a right not to belong to a trade union (see Appendix).

266. This Section examines the closed shop and the related practices to which it has given rise. In each case it considers the recent attempts to correct their unacceptable features through legislation and the further proposals which have been made for changes in the law.

The closed shop

267. In the 1970s the closed shop was affected by three successive statutes. The Industrial Relations Act 1971 declared some closed shop agreements void and provided a right for employees not to belong to a union. It created the alternative of an "agency shop" for registered unions. This enabled those who did not wish to be associated with the policies of the union and conscientious objectors to remain non-union members but to contribute to union funds or to a charity. The Act met considerable resistance from trade unions and in practice its closed shop provisions were circumvented by many employers and unions. The closed shop continued much as before.

268. The Trade Union and Labour Relations Acts 1974 and 1976 reversed the position of the 1971 Act. Under the 1974 Act dismissal for non-membership of a trade union in a closed shop was stated to be fair unless the employee genuinely objected to membership on religious or any other reasonable grounds. In 1976 such grounds were narrowed to those of religious objections only. These provisions encouraged the spread of the closed shop and prompted in turn renewed concern about the individual's freedom of choice and also specifically about the impact of the closed shop on editorial freedom in the press. In 1976 the TUC set up an Independent Review Committee to consider appeals from individuals who had lost their job as a result of being excluded or expelled from union membership and in 1979 issued guidance on the closed shop. This, amongst other things, reminded unions that closed shop agreements should be flexible and that many made provision for conscientious objectors; and it advised them that, in seeking 100 per cent union membership, they should adopt approaches which placed the main emphasis on persuading workers of the benefits of trade union membership.

269. In 1976 a British Rail employee who lost his job as a result of refusing to join a union following the introduction of a new closed shop agreement between British Rail and the National Union of Railwaymen, was found by an industrial tribunal to have been fairly dismissed under the 1976 Act. He and two colleagues who had been similarly dismissed took their case to the European Commission on Human Rights. The Commission reported the 1976 Act to be in breach of the European Convention of Human Rights and has referred the matter to the European Court on Human Rights for determination.

Effects of the Employment Act

270. The Employment Act 1980 has provided new protection for individuals against dismissal (or action short of dismissal) for non-union membership in a closed shop where:

- the employee genuinely objects on grounds of conscience or other deeply held personal conviction to being a member of any trade union whatsoever or of a particular trade union;

- the employee belonged to the class of employee covered by the closed shop agreement before it took effect, and has not been a union member since;

- the closed shop agreement came into effect after 15 August 1980 and has not been approved by at least 80 per cent of those to be covered voting in a secret ballot.

Had these provisions been in force in 1976, the Government believes that the case now before the European Court would not have arisen. The Act also gives a remedy for an employee against being unreasonably excluded or expelled from a union where a closed shop agreement applies to the job he seeks, or in which he is already employed.

271. The Government has also produced a Code of Practice on Closed Shop Agreements and Arrangements which has received the approval of both Houses of Parliament and became effective on 17 December 1980. Its purpose is to explain the law and to give authoritative guidance on good practice. In proceedings before any court or industrial tribunal the provisions of the Code must be taken into account where they are relevant.

272. These measures should bring about important changes in the operation of closed shop agreements. But the issue of the closed shop understandably arouses strong feelings and there are those who believe that the law should go further. Several suggestions have, in consequence, been put forward for circumscribing or eliminating altogether unions' ability to press for closed shop agreements and their enforcement. The main ways in which this might be done are considered below.

(i) Voiding of closed shop agreements

273. One suggestion is to make closed shop agreements void (ie in effect to declare closed shop agreements unlawful). This would make any such agreement unenforceable at law. Since, however, such collective agreements are generally not enforced or enforceable at law, it would probably be necessary also to provide that any action to secure or enforce such agreements would be unlawful.

274. It is argued in favour of this proposal that it gives the clearest and most comprehensive expression to disapproval of closed shops and is in line with the law on the subject in the majority of other European countries. It would be equally binding on employers and trade unions who wanted to conclude closed shop agreements. It would, therefore, give relief, it is argued, not only to all individual employees who did not want to join a union, but also to potential recruits for employment in a closed shop.

275. Against this it can be argued that the closed shop is so established a feature of our industrial relations system that it would not disappear. Indeed it can be argued that, as in the years following the Industrial Relations Act 1971, *de facto* closed shop agreements would continue to be established as a matter of practice and to operate against the interests of individual employees.

(ii) Periodic review

276. The closed shop Code (paragraphs 42–46) outlines what is good practice in reviewing existing closed shops. It suggests that reviews should take place every few years. If, as a result of such a review, the employer and union favour continuing the closed shop agreement or arrangement, the Code says they "should ensure that it has continued support among the current employees to whom it applies. Where no secret ballot has previously been held—or where one has not been held for a long time—it would be appropriate to use one to test opinion" (paragraph 45).

277. It has been proposed that over and above guidance on good practice there should be a legal requirement that all closed shop agreements be subject to a periodic review of support among the employees they cover or that it should be unfair to dismiss an employee who is not a union member unless there have been periodic review ballots which show continued support for any closed shop agreement. Alternatively a review ballot might not be required automatically, but a given percentage (eg 20 per cent) of those covered by the closed shop should be able to request a review periodically.

278. Those who argue against any new legal requirement of this kind point to the disturbance to industrial relations which a statutory requirement to review could entail. During consultations on the closed shop Code many employers, as well as trade unions, were unhappy even about including advice on periodic reviews in a Code of Practice. They argued that it would enable splinter, and possibly militant, groups to undermine established representational arrangements and that employers could be faced with the consequences of inter and intra-union disputes. Some employers argued that they could be relied upon to take proper account of obvious and significant dissatisfaction with the closed shop and that the initiative for review and its timing should rest with management.

279. Against this it can be argued that it is no more than normal good practice for agreements between management and unions to be reviewed regularly and that closed shop agreements are no different from other agreements in this respect. It can be argued indeed that it is particularly important that there should be regular reviews of closed shop agreements, because of the threat they may pose to an individual's job and livelihood if he does not wish to join a union. Unless there are regular reviews, it is argued, once a closed shop agreement is established, employees in practice become locked into it, with the result that the closed shop becomes a still more pervasive feature of British industrial relations.

69

(iii) Unreasonable operation of a closed shop

280. It has also been suggested that employees and applicants for employment should be protected by creating a new statutory right against the unreasonable operation of a closed shop. The Code of Practice on the closed shop gives guidance as to the way in which a closed shop agreement should be entered into and operated. If such a right were created industrial tribunals would have to take the Code into account if they considered it relevant but it would not necessarily be decisive.

281. Against this suggestion it is argued that such a right would be ill-defined and uncertain in effect and that it would thrust industrial tribunals into the difficult area of deciding what it was reasonable to include in, or exclude from, agreements of this kind and how those agreements should be operated.

Related practices

282. It was noted in paragraph 265 that the closed shop has sometimes been used by unions against non-union companies and their employees. This has usually meant employees in highly unionised companies "blacking" goods and materials from non-union sources or, alternatively, refusing to allow employees from other companies on to a site or into a factory without a union card. Such practices are used most often in those industries, such as construction, where contracting out of work is common and where new technology and shifting patterns of work have meant that jobs traditionally done by union members in an industry can now be done outside the industry by non-union employees.

283. Section 18 of the Employment Act 1980 has already dealt with a relatively recent development in the use of industrial action against non-union firms. It has removed immunity from the organisers of industrial action which has the purpose of compelling workers to join a trade union. It is designed to deal with the kind of coercive recruitment practices used by the Society of Lithographic Artists, Designers, Engravers and Process Workers (SLADE) in the art and advertising industry, described in the report of Mr Andrew Leggatt QC in October 1979.

284. The Leggatt report found that SLADE had instructed its members at the printing houses to black goods and materials from non-unionised art studios, photographic laboratories and advertising agencies, in order to compel the employees in those companies to become SLADE members. It concluded:

> "When conventional methods of recruitment failed SLADE embarked on a deliberate plan to 'organise' the industry . . . It was conducted without any regard to the feelings, interests or welfare of the prospective recruits . . . Often a closed shop was imposed against the wishes not only of the employer but of all the employees . . .
>
> Where employees are coerced into joining a union against the alternative of being put out of business, the union subscription is bound to look like payment for a licence to work or 'protection' money". (paragraphs 200–201).

70

285. Section 18 deals with this kind of practice. A person who calls industrial action in order to compel workers to join a particular trade union (or one of two or more particular trade unions) is no longer protected by immunity if the workers being induced to join a union work for a different employer and at different premises from the employees taking the industrial action.

286. The Section has been criticised on the grounds that it focuses too narrowly on coercive recruitment practices. It is argued that similar practices involving industrial action against non-union companies should also be tackled. Three in particular are discussed below:

    (i) the refusal to handle work from non-union companies;

    (ii) the refusal to work with non-union labour; and

    (iii) the practice adopted by some organisations of inserting clauses in contracts requiring contractors to employ only union labour on the contract.

Refusal to handle work from non-union companies

287. Probably the best known examples of union members refusing to handle work from non-union companies are provided by the printing industry where the closed shop is long established. The main craft unions in the industry, the National Graphical Association (NGA) and SLADE have seen the development of new technology as a challenge to their traditional craft-based structure. They have responded by blacking work from non-approved sources.

288. At its most organised the blacking is based on what is known as a "fair list" of those companies which the union regards as having satisfactory terms and conditions of employment. To get on the list a company will usually have to recognise the union for collective bargaining purposes and to conclude a closed shop agreement with it. The list is circulated to union branches and updated regularly through union journals or circulars: branch officials are under standing instructions not to handle work from companies not on the list.

289. The extent to which refusal to handle non-union work is affected by Section 18 of the Employment Act 1980 depends on the purpose for which such action is taken. Where, as in the SLADE case, companies are blacked with the purpose of compelling their workers to join a particular trade union, the organisers of the blacking have no immunity under the Act and an injunction may be sought against them. However, it is arguable that the practice is more commonly used, not to compel the workers in such companies to join a union, but to prevent them from doing work which has traditionally been the preserve of union members. In such cases, where the purpose of the action was not to compel union membership, its organisers would continue to have immunity.

290. The question is whether immunity should be removed from all industrial action of this kind, whether or not its purpose is specifically to compel union membership. The practical effects of such a change would depend

71

on the reactions to it from management and unions. It would protect non-union firms to the extent that they continued to receive contracts from listed companies and found those contracts interfered with by blacking. It would not, however, prevent unions drawing up fair lists and concluding agreements with listed companies that they should not do business with non-listed firms. To the extent that such agreements were concluded, non-listed firms would continue to be at a disadvantage. To protect them against this would require further provision to make such agreements unlawful. This is discussed in paragraphs 295-302 below.

(iv) Refusing to work with non-union labour

291. The parallel practice of refusing to work alongside non-union labour is particularly common in industries where there is a long tradition of trade union membership, as in the docks, and where there is a high level of sub-contracting as in certain parts of the civil engineering and construction industries. But the widespread use of sub-contractors for maintenance work means that almost all types of firm are liable to be involved in a dispute of this nature. As with the refusal to handle non-union goods, the purpose of refusing to work with non-union labour can be either to extend trade union membership or to defend areas of work traditionally done by union members. But it can also operate with no particular objective in view other than what might be accounted a political demonstration on the part of a highly organised working group of its belief that full trade union membership is essential.

292. Section 18 of the Employment Act 1980 does not apply where the workers taking the industrial action and the workers against whom the action is taken work at the same place of work. It has been suggested that the words "at the same place" should be removed from Section 18, so that it covers the situation in which the two groups of workers concerned are working at the same place. This would remove immunity in those cases where the purpose of refusing to work with non-union employees was to compel those workers to join a particular trade union. But it would not cover action which was designed to persuade an employer to replace a non-union contractor with a contractor who employed only union labour or which sought simply to require the "blacked" employees to produce a union card without specifying membership of a particular trade union.

293. One other effect of this proposal would be to make it much more difficult for unions to organise primary industrial action among employees at a place of work to force the employer of those employees to concede a closed shop. This is because primary action in a dispute about the establishment of a closed shop might very well fall into the category of action to compel union membership.

294. It is clear that the practical industrial relations consequences of removing immunity from this practice need special consideration. The refusal to work with non-union labour is not always simply the result of hostility against those who do not hold a union card. In some industries, particularly on some construction sites, the union card is regarded as an

72

assurance to those working on site that the newcomer has reached acceptable standards of safety and training. In some other cases, whether with justification or not, union members have come to associate the non-union employer with poor wages and conditions which they fear will undercut them, thereby jeopardising their jobs. Where these beliefs are held, an attempt to challenge a refusal to work with non-union employees may not prove persuasive. In these circumstances, a civil action by the employer of the excluded employees, or by the other employer, might not provide an effective remedy.

Union labour only contract clauses

295. Both the refusal of employees to handle work from non-union sources and to work with non-union labour are sometimes reinforced by what are known as union labour only contract clauses. An employer who is subcontracting work puts a clause in the contract requiring the contractor to use only union labour to fulfil it. This means, for example, that if the contractor sends non-union employees to do the work in question he is in breach of contract and may either lose the contract altogether or be sued for the breach.

296. Union labour only contract clauses are relatively common in the civil engineering and construction industries. They are generally used by employers who have concluded closed shop agreements with their unions and in doing so have undertaken to ensure that no work is contracted out to non-union companies. The contract clause is seen in such cases by both employers and unions as an insurance against the potentially disruptive effects on industrial relations of introducing a non-union worker on to a site. In defence of this practice, clients of contractors can argue that it is almost always they, and not the contractors themselves, who suffer as a result of such disruption.

297. These clauses have been strongly criticised by the contractors and their representatives. They are seen as an insidious way of spreading the closed shop and as threatening particularly the commercial viability of small, non-union companies whose employees have no interest in joining the union. In effect, it is argued, such companies can face the choice between persuading their non-union employees to become union members or replacing them with union members as an alternative to being put out of business altogether.

298. The Government has already made clear its dislike of this practice in the debates on the Employment Bill and it has taken a number of steps to discourage it. It has sought to dissuade employers in the private and public sectors from using such clauses and has requested the support of the CBI. The Code of Practice on the closed shop states that there should be no attempt, by formal or informal means, to impose a requirement of union membership on the employees of contractors or suppliers and customers by anyone who has concluded a closed shop agreement. Moreover Section 10 of the Employment Act, which enables a contractor, who is compelled to dismiss one of his non-union employees because of a union

73

labour only contract clause and is subsequently involved in unfair dismissal proceedings as a result of the dismissal, to join in the proceedings the client who has insisted on the clause being inserted. In turn, that employer may join in the proceedings a union or other person who, by industrial action or its threat, caused him to insist on the union labour only requirement.

299. These measures should help to discourage adoption of union labour only contract clauses. The question is whether further measures are needed. Representatives of the contractors have argued that such clauses should be declared null and void in legislation so that, even if they continue to appear in contracts, they cannot be enforced at law.

300. The potential effects of this are uncertain. A reduction in the number of contracts with union labour only clauses could certainly be expected. But it can be argued that many organisations would no longer place contracts with known non-union companies, or that they would require contractors to send only union labour to fulfil a contract, without actually putting such a requirement into the written contract. There are already examples of such informal understandings about the use of union labour which never appear in a contract. The understanding is effective because the contractor knows that, if he sends non-union labour on any occasion, he is unlikely to receive further work from that client in the future.

301. A provision declaring contract clauses null and void would also have no effect on industrial action against the non-union employer. This has led to suggestions that such a provision should be supported by the removal of immunity from industrial action which takes the form of refusal to work with non-union labour. (This is discussed in paragraphs 291-294 above). But again this would not necessarily prevent informal arrangements between employers to ensure that work on a site or in a factory was done only by union members.

302. It has also been suggested that the problem of discrimination against non-union firms in the awarding of contracts should be dealt with by a provision making such discrimination unlawful. It must be doubtful, however, whether such a provision could be operated effectively. Many factors govern the award of contracts and it could often be very difficult for the disappointed contractor to prove discrimination on these grounds. Furthermore, the effect of making employers liable for costly litigation because of alleged discrimination could be to discourage them from using contractors at all.

Conclusion

303. There remains great public concern about the closed shop and about industrial action against non-union employees and companies. Any practice which makes the holding of a job and the continuation of business dependent on the holding of a union card cannot be convincingly defended.

304. On the other hand, the closed shop is a major feature of our industrial relations system with a long history. There are practical limitations

on the extent to which such long standing practices can be eradicated by law and there is inevitably some uncertainty as to what would be the effects of trying to do so. The Employment Act 1980, which came into effect only in August 1980, has increased the protection for individuals in a closed shop and removed immunity from industrial action to compel union membership.

305. The Government would welcome views on

(a) whether further changes in legislation affecting the closed shop and related practices are desirable at this stage; and

(b) whether such further changes would be likely to prove effective.

· H PROTECTING THE COMMUNITY

306. Recurring mention has been made in this Green Paper of the problem of protecting the community as a whole against the potentially damaging effects of industrial action without restricting the freedoms of trade unions and individual workers to an unacceptable extent. It has to be recognised that there is no absolute protection which can be given to the community without outlawing industrial action altogether. The freedom to strike imposes on any society which upholds it a potential liability to sustain damage. Therefore, the community must be able to count on trade unions and individual workers to exercise their power with restraint and responsibility. But over and above this, Governments have a duty, when the interests of the community are put at risk, to take whatever steps are necessary to ensure that access to essential goods and services is protected and the hardship inflicted on the community is limited as much as possible.

307. The discussion so far has centred on where the line should be drawn. Some changes in the law to provide better protection to others engaged in industry and the community were made by the Employment Act: other possibilities have been canvassed elsewhere in this Chapter. The question considered here, however, is whether there comes a point at which the interests of the nation must override the freedom to take industrial action in order to protect the community and the national interest.

308. This Section is not concerned with the wholly exceptional circumstances of a war, when a manifest emergency exists and special considerations apply. The main concern here is whether there are circumstances in which industrial action poses such a threat to the national interest that special provisions are needed to deal with it. The question is considered from two points of view:

(a) the general question of industrial action which creates a national emergency; and

(b) industrial action by workers in essential services.

National emergencies

309. The Government already has power under the Emergency Powers Acts 1920 and 1964 to deal with the consequences of an emergency, whether or not it is created by industrial action. The 1920 Act enables a Royal Proclamation of Emergency to be issued where it appears that there is likely to be interference with the supply and distribution of food, water, fuel, light or the means of locomotion, such as to deprive a substantial portion of the community of "the essentials of life". This, in turn, permits the making of regulations for securing essential supplies "and for any other purposes essential to the public safety and the life of the community".

310. The 1920 Act contains restrictions on the Government's power to declare a state of emergency and to issue regulations. These are primarily designed to ensure that Parliament is informed immediately an emergency has been declared, and its approval of Emergency Regulations is sought within seven days and renewed at monthly intervals thereafter. But the most important in the context of the present discussion is the one concerning industrial action. This specifically prohibits the Government, notwithstanding the emergency, from issuing a regulation under the Act making it an offence to strike or to picket peacefully.

311. It is argued that the existing powers enable the Government to take immediate action to deal with the emergency while protecting, at the same time, the freedom to strike and to picket peacefully. On this view, it is the only kind of action which the Government can realistically and reasonably take in such circumstances. Any attempt to make the strike itself unlawful would, it is argued, be unworkable and unenforceable.

312. Against this, however, is the view that the present law enables the Government to deal only with the immediate *consequences* of an emergency and that additional powers are needed to enable it to deal with the industrial action itself. Two possibilities for change are most commonly suggested:

(a) a power for the Government to delay the strike by order while further negotiations are undertaken. This is sometimes known as a "statutory cooling off period";

(b) a power for the Government to declare unlawful a strike which threatens the national interest.

A statutory cooling off period

313. An example of a statutory cooling off period is provided by the Industrial Relations Act 1971. Under the Act the Secretary of State for Employment had the power to seek an order from the NIRC restraining a union, employer or any named person from calling, inducing or financing industrial action when:

"the industrial action in question has caused, or (as the case may be) would cause, an interruption in the supply of goods or in the provision of services of such a nature, or on such a scale, as to be likely—

(a) to be gravely injurious to the national economy, to imperil national security or to create a serious risk of public disorder, or

76

(*b*) to endanger the lives of a substantial number of persons, or to
expose a substantial number of persons to serious risk of disease
or personal injury''. (Section 138).

314. The NIRC could make such an order for a period of up to 60 days
during which all the parties concerned were expected to do everything possible to effect a settlement. Under the 1971 Act there was also a provision
which enabled the Secretary of State, if circumstances warranted, to seek
a further order for a secret ballot of the workers concerned. If, at the
end of the cooling off period or after a ballot no settlement was reached,
then the strike could resume. The Government had no further statutory
power to intervene to prevent it.

315. The principle behind the provision was not that the Government
should have the power to ban strikes, but that it should be given a delaying
power during which there could be further negotiations to find a settlement.
The provision was only used once: in the 1972 national rail dispute. The
Secretary of State for Employment successfully sought orders for a cooling
off period during which the industrial action was suspended, and then for
a ballot. The orders were observed. The result of the ballot was, however,
an endorsement of the industrial action which was then resumed (see paragraph 250).

316. The model for the 1971 Act provisions were the emergency provisions of the Taft Hartley Act in the USA. Under this Act the President
can ask the Attorney-General to seek a cooling off period of up to 80 days
if, in his opinion, a strike affecting an entire industry or a substantial part
of it will, if h is permitted, ''imperil the national health or safety''. There
is also provision for a ballot to be held towards the end of the cooling
off period on the employer's last offer. Again, as under the Industrial Relations Act 1971, if the employees reject the offer, the strike may go ahead
though the President may then submit a report to Congress recommending
further action.

317. The experience of the working of the Taft Hartley Act is that, though
the cooling off period is usually effective in suspending the strike, the subsequent ballot almost always results in an endorsement of the original strike.
During its 33 years the Act has been used in 35 national emergency disputes.
In the 24 cases where injunctions against the strike have been granted there
is only one clear case of the injunction being defied by the workers on
strike. In the resulting ballots, covering 163 bargaining units, the employer's
last offer has been rejected by the workers in 155 cases and accepted in
only 8.

318. This suggests that in some circumstances it may be counter-productive for the Government to become involved in trying to find a settlement
and that in fact the ballot of workers is regarded less as a vote on the
employer's offer than as a vote of confidence in their union and in the
Government's handling of the dispute. It can be argued that one advantage
of this process is that it does delay the damaging effects of the strike for

77

a period. But, if there is no settlement at the end of that period, the strike is back where it started with an endorsement in a secret ballot which may make a settlement even more difficult to negotiate. A statutory cooling off period and a provision for ballots are not, of course, mutually exclusive. American experience, for example, suggests that a cooling off period will not necessarily be made more effective by requiring a ballot during it.

A power to make strikes unlawful

319. The lack of success of cooling off periods has led to suggestions in Britain for giving the Government a power to declare unlawful strikes which create or threaten a national emergency. It is suggested that the simplest way of doing this would be to remove the restriction in the 1920 Act on the Government's power to make a strike or peaceful picketing an offence by regulation or to create a separate power for the Government to seek an order from the courts banning a strike. Such a power could be subject to regular Parliamentary approval as are the powers under the Emergency Powers Act 1920; alternatively, the power could be exercised only on application to the courts for an order to make a strike unlawful.

320. The major objection to such a proposal is that even with these safeguards it places in the hands of the executive a considerable power to restrict strikes and undermines basic liberties in a way which many would regard as unacceptable. The question is whether such a power can ever be justified outside the wholly exceptional circumstances of a war. The Emergency Powers Act 1920, which has formed the basis of the Government's powers for 60 years, is drafted on the basis that a power to declare strikes unlawful is not justified. The Act has been accepted by all Governments throughout that period and the powers it provides have been used by both major political parties when in Government.

321. There are also two important considerations which apply to this and to all other proposals for special emergency provisions. The first relates to the definition of a national emergency: the second to the sanctions which would be applied against those who refused to comply with an order suspending or outlawing the strike.

Definition of an emergency

322. When war breaks out or a natural disaster occurs, it is easy to agree that an emergency has been created. When it is a question of industrial action it is much more difficult to find an acceptable definition. Three definitions have been described above:

- interference with the supply of food, water, fuel and light or with transport and depriving the community of "the essentials of life". (Emergency Powers Act 1920);

- a strike affecting a whole industry or substantial part of it which endangers the "national health or safety" (the US Taft Hartley Act 1947); and

78

- industrial action which is gravely injurious to the national economy, imperils national security, creates a serious risk of disorder, endangers the lives of a substantial number of people or exposes a substantial number to serious risk of disease or personal injury (Industrial Relations Act 1971).

323. Some elements of these definitions are common. Most people, for example, would accept that action which puts lives at risk or imperils national security constitutes an emergency. Action of this type is rare, although industrial action has sometimes been experienced which cannot be justified on moral grounds, for example when essential supplies and services to the sick have been disrupted. In general workers who are in a position to endanger life or threaten security either do not go on strike, or if they do so, ensure that essential services are maintained. The community has the right to expect nothing less. In our society the force of public opinion remains a potent factor.

324. There is likely to be very little agreement, however, on how far these definitions should cover industrial action which damages the national economy or the interests of the community. It can be argued that such action is in a quite different category from that which threatens life or the security of the nation and that, while the effects of some strikes on the national economy are very serious indeed and deeply damaging to society as a whole, they are unlikely to be so acute as to constitute an emergency sufficient to justify giving the Government such sweeping powers. Furthermore, in our present society there will be always considerable difficulties in drawing a line around industrial action which is not damaging to the economy or to society. So interdependent and interconnected are firms and industries that there is almost no major strike which will not ultimately affect the interests of the economy or community as a whole. It is arguable indeed that a power for the Government to declare strikes unlawful if they threaten the community or the national economy would put at risk almost every major strike which occurred.

Sanctions

325. It can also be argued that the wider the coverage of an emergency power, the less easy it will be to enforce. Experience suggests that people are prepared to forego liberties if they genuinely believe that the interests of the nation are seriously threatened. On the other hand, a power which is seen as a way of using an emergency so as to restrict the freedom to strike is much more likely to be disobeyed.

326. This raises the question of what sanction there could be against someone who disobeyed an order to stop a strike. The removal of immunities from the organisers of industrial action seems an inadequate remedy in the case of a national emergency. It would enable an employer to sue the organisers of the industrial action for an injunction or damages but the community as a whole would be protected only if an employer decided

79

to bring such a private action. It would not provide the Government itself with any direct means of intervening to stop the strike or to protect the community.

327. It is instructive to look at the sanctions employed by the Industrial Relations Act 1971 to enforce the order for the cooling off period. The order was to be made against the person or organisation which had called the strike. If that person or organisation disobeyed the order by refusing to rescind its instruction to strike, then the NIRC could impose a fine for contempt of court. There was no power, however, to force individuals to go back to work. If the strike continued, even though the union had instructed its members to go back to work, there was nothing the Government or the NIRC could do about it. This was recognition of the fact that, while it is possible to penalise a person for breaking his employment contract, it is very difficult to force him to perform the contract if he is determined not to do so.[1]

328. The only alternative to making the strike organiser liable to fines for breach of an order seems to be to make a strike in defiance of an emergency regulation a criminal offence. This would make both the organiser and the individual strikers liable to criminal prosecution if they disobeyed and continued the strike.

329. Mass prosecution of strikers can hardly, however, be regarded as a practical proposition. This is illustrated by Sir Harold Emmerson's evidence to the Donovan Commission (reproduced in full in Appendix 6 to the Commission's report) on the Government's unsuccessful attempts to prosecute 4,000 striking miners at the Betteshanger Colliery in Kent in 1941. This, and the general experience of proscribing strikes in the Second World War, led the Donovan Commission to comment on "the fruitlessness of the use of penal sanctions for the purpose of enforcing industrial peace". Even in wartime it proved impossible to prevent strikes altogether by making strikers liable to criminal prosecution.

Restrictions on workers in essential industries

330. An alternative approach would be to make it unlawful for certain key groups of workers to take industrial action. This, it is argued, would have the advantage of providing permanent protection to the community without placing unacceptable discretionary powers in the hands of the Government. It can be further argued that it is not an unreasonable condition of employment in an essential service for the employee to be required to waive his right to abrogate that contract at will if the consequence is to threaten the continued function of that service with grave effects on the country.

[1] This reflects a principle of British law, which is now enshrined in Section 16 of the Trade Union and Labour Relations Act 1974, that no one should be compelled by order of a court to carry out a contract of employment or personal service.

331. The only current examples of workers for whom strikes are illegal are the police, merchant seaman when they are at sea and the armed forces. In each case, however, there are arguments of public order, security and safety which make it difficult to draw any general lessons for other industries.

332. Until 1971 it was also a criminal offence for employees of gas, water and electricity undertakings to break their employment contracts believing that the consequence would be to deprive consumers of the whole or the greater part of their supply. This meant in effect that it was illegal for employees in these industries to go on strike unless they gave due notice (usually a week) of their intention to break their contracts of employment. The Donovan Commission commented that the main value of such a provision was that it imposed a short period of delay before work ceased. It also found, however, that the provisions had been little used. In his evidence to the Commission the then Chairman of the Gas Council could recall only one case in which proceedings under it had been taken. That was in 1950 but the proceedings were withdrawn following a conviction under the emergency powers regulations then in force.

333. In short, in the few cases in Great Britain where the law restricts strikes by key groups of workers it has been little used. Though there have been disturbing exceptions, in general workers in key sectors have exercised their considerable power to disrupt the community with restraint. As was noted earlier, if they have taken industrial action at all they have usually maintained essential services and supplies. Against this background the central question is whether the imposition of legal restrictions on the ability of such groups to strike at this stage in the development of their industries is likely to be fruitful. Before taking such a step a number of important considerations would have to be taken into account.

334. First, there would be great difficulty in deciding which groups of workers should be chosen and on what criteria. There are clearly dangers in going too wide or appearing to be inequitable. There are many views on which groups should be restricted but very little agreement, not least amongst those industries which are most frequently mentioned. As was noted in paragraph 324 above, the interdependent nature of industry means that a case can now be made for regarding a strike by most groups of workers as threatening essential services or supplies.

335. Secondly, the likely effects on industrial relations must be assessed. No group of workers would welcome the removal of a freedom to strike which has been hard won and long held. There would be the possibility of resistance and even industrial disruption if the law were changed on an issue of deeply held principle: this might be supported by trade unionists not directly affected by such restrictions.

336. Finally, the problems of enforcement discussed above arise here too. The removal of immunities seems an inadequate means of tackling industrial action by strikers who create an emergency because, as was noted

in paragraph 341, it would make the protection of the community dependent on an individual employer bringing a private action. The alternative, however, is to bring in the criminal law with all the problems of enforcement which that would entail.

337. These considerations suggest that there might be very great difficulties in making strikes by key groups of workers illegal. It is possible to argue that the most effective way of making progress on this question is through voluntary "no strike" agreements between management and unions in those sectors of industry where strikes might threaten the national interest.

Conclusion

338. This is a sensitive and difficult area in which arguments of fundamental principle and practice must be carefully weighed. The Government would welcome views on the proposals for changes discussed in this Section.

CHAPTER 4

AN ALTERNATIVE SYSTEM OF POSITIVE RIGHTS

339. The last Chapter discussed possible changes in the law which might be made to the existing system of immunities which provides the legal framework for industrial relations in this country. This Chapter considers whether and how the immunities could be converted into a system of positive rights, similar to those operating in a number of other countries.

340. The Chapter is concerned primarily with the law as it relates to strikes and other industrial action. It concentrates, therefore, on the possibility of replacing the immunities provided by Sections 13 and 14 of the Trade Union and Labour Relations Acts 1974 and 1976, and by the Employment Act 1980, by a positive rights equivalent. It is not primarily concerned with other rights, such as the right to associate and to join a trade union which are common features of other systems, except in so far as they may be considered an essential adjunct to a positive right to strike.

341. The Chapter discusses the main characteristics of an alternative system based on the positive right to strike and in so doing identifies the main decisions that would be required and difficulties to be resolved. Its purpose is not to consider whether, in converting to a positive rights system, any changes of the kind discussed in the last Chapter should be made at the same time, though this question inevitably arises at certain points. Its purpose is of a more legal character: to discuss what would be involved in changing from our present system based on immunities to a system based on a positive right to strike. To provide a background for this discussion the Chapter first considers how far the concept of positive legal rights is already present in the system of labour law in this country.

Positive rights in British labour law

342. The common law itself, which provides the guiding precepts for our whole legal system, comprises in fact a series of fundamental rights and duties which, unless abrogated by legislation or sometimes by contract, govern all relationships including those at the workplace. As has been seen, however, these fundamental rights are not sufficient to guarantee the legality of trade union activity. It is because the common law operated to make associations of workers and concerted industrial action unlawful, that a system of immunities from legal processes at common law has developed. Indeed, simply to repeal the immunities and to return to the common law could make it virtually impossible for trade unions to exist and operate lawfully at all.

343. Positive legal rights have also been introduced into British labour law by statute. Three examples may be cited:
  (i) a number of Acts of Parliament, particularly during the last decade, have conferred positive employment rights on individuals. Some of these have simply strengthened or confirmed rights recognised at

common law (eg the right to notice before termination of contract); others have introduced new rights on which the common law is silent (eg rights in relation to guaranteed pay and maternity);

(ii) the Employment Protection Act 1975 established a number of trade union rights (eg the right to information for collective bargaining purposes, the right to be consulted about a redundancy), again in areas where the common law was silent;

(iii) the Industrial Relations Act 1971 established a number of legal rights including, for the first time, the right to join and not to join a trade union; Section 1 also contained a description of the "guiding principles" on which the provisions of the Act were based. These included the principle of free association of workers in independent trade unions and the principle of collective bargaining "freely conducted on behalf of workers and employers and with due regard to the general interests of the community". The Act was repealed in 1974.

In addition, a number of international conventions and treaties to which the United Kingdom is a party have established basic employment rights. The European Convention for the Protection of Human Rights and Fundamental Freedom, for example, guarantees an employee's right to freedom of association, including in particular the right to join or form a trade union.

344. However, these examples of existing positive rights provide only limited practical guidance on how to convert a system of immunities into a system of positive rights. There are two reasons for this. First, none of these rights is concerned directly with the law as it relates to industrial action. Secondly, none of these rights has been introduced in areas where there has previously existed an immunity from the operation of the common law. In general, they have dealt only with areas where there are already common law rights which needed enlarging or where the common law is silent altogether.

345. In short, the introduction of positive rights into the law relating to strikes and industrial action in Great Britain would be an entirely novel step. It would represent a fundamental change from the legal system based on immunities which has developed over the last 100 years. This raises major issues which cannot, logically, be isolated from the question whether there should be some general form of Bill of Rights. This is, of course, a wider question than the subject matter of this Green Paper.

Main characteristics of a positive right in relation to strikes

346. The following would appear to be the main matters to be resolved in adopting a system of positive rights.

(i) A right to strike or a right to organise a strike?

347. Most legal systems based on positive rights start with a statement of fundamental rights which forms the basis for all subsequent labour law.

These basic rights are sometimes contained in the Constitution itself; some-times they are to be found in statute. They almost all' include in one form or another the right of employees to strike though, as will be seen, this right has usually been limited by subsequent legislation.

348. As the previous Chapter showed, the nearest equivalent to the right to strike in Great Britain is the immunities from actions in tort under Sections 13 or 14 of the Trade Union and Labour Relations Acts 1974 and 1976 as restricted by the Employment Act 1980. These immunities, however, protect the *organisers* of industrial action, whether they be individuals, trade unions or employers' associations. There is no immunity for the employees who actually take the industrial action; if they do so in breach of their contracts of employment they may be sued in contract.

349. The exact equivalent of the current immunity in a positive rights system would not, therefore, be a right to strike, but a right to organise a strike. This is not a concept which is recognised in other countries; in most countries the right to organise a strike is held to be implicit in the right to strike itself and other protective rights such as the right to take part in trade union activities. If, therefore, there were to be a positive right in relation to industrial action in Great Britain, it is arguable that it should be a right to strike rather than a right to organise a strike.

350. It would also be necessary to decide whether such a right should override the law of contract and enable those who go on strike in breach of their contracts of employment to do so without fear of being sued by their employers or being dismissed. French law, for example, regards a strike as suspending the individual contract of employment. In contrast, US law states that a strike during the renegotiation of a collective agreement breaks the employment contract and allows the employer to dismiss the strikers and to take on replacement workers.

351. There is also the question of whether a right to strike implies a right not to strike. This does not appear to be an issue in other countries, but it would be relevant to the situation in this country where unions discipline members for refusing to follow their instructions to strike. If there were a right not to strike the question would arise whether such disciplinary action was legal.

(ii) The right to lock-out

352. The immunities apply equally to employers and employers' associ-ations who organise a lock-out. This suggests that in a positive rights system the right to strike might need to be matched with a corresponding right to lock-out.

' An exception is West Germany where the Constitution of 1949 is silent on the subject of the right to strike. The courts and subsequent legislation seem, however, to operate on the basis that a *de facto* right to strike exists.

353. The right of an employer to lock-out his employees is recognised in most countries, though often as a result of judicial decision rather than in the Constitution or in statute. An exception is Sweden where the right to strike and to lock-out appear alongside each other in Article 5 of the Swedish Constitution:

> "Any trade union and any employer or association of employers shall have the right to take strike or lock-out actions or any similar measures, except as otherwise provided by law or ensuing from a contract".

354. The same questions as those described in paragraphs 347–350 would arise in relation to a right to lock-out. Should there, for example, be a right to lock-out or a right to *organise* a lock-out? Should an employer exercising the right of lock-out be liable for breaking employment contracts?

(iii) Definition and limitation of the right to strike

355. A right to strike or lock-out by itself would leave almost unlimited scope for industrial action. It would therefore be necessary to limit that right in a number of ways.

356. In most other countries the basic right to strike has been limited by subsequent legislation. These limitations fall into six main categories, five of which have parallels in the existing law in Great Britain. These parallels have been considered in Chapter 3. As part of a change to a positive rights system it would be necessary to determine precisely what restrictions should be placed on the right to strike in respect of:

(a) secondary action (Section B of Chapter 3);

(b) picketing (Section C);

(c) political strikes (Section D);

(d) strikes in breach of contract (Section E); and

(e) special groups of essential workers (Section I1).

357. The sixth category of limitation of the basic right to strike relates to the legality of industrial action short of a strike. In most systems the right to take action short of a strike (eg a work to rule or "go slow") derives from the right to strike itself and is not specified separately. In some countries (such as Sweden) action short of a strike is covered by a formula such as "strike action or other similar measures". In others (eg France) it has been specifically declared unlawful. British law recognises no such distinctions: either the contract of employment is broken or it is not.

358. In respect of each of these restrictions it would be necessary to decide whether it should be defined so as precisely to reproduce present British law or whether any changes (eg those discussed in Chapter 3) should be made.

359. This is not an exhaustive list of the decisions and problems which would be involved in limiting a right to strike. But it illustrates the extent

to which a positive right to strike would need detailed definition and limitation in legislation. It is important to note that, wherever the law was silent on a particular point, the right to strike would apply and, wherever this created uncertainty in the law, it would be for the courts to decide what the right to strike meant.

(iv) Corresponding obligations

360. Another way in which rights may be defined or circumscribed is by the obligations which are placed on others not to interfere with them. In other systems this question arises most clearly in relation to rights other than the right to strike. The right to join a trade union, for example, is usually supported by an obligation on an employer not to prevent someone from joining a union. Equally the right of employees to bargain which is written into some systems imposes a correlative duty on an employer to bargain in good faith with representatives of employees.

361. There are not many circumstances in which interference with the right to strike is likely to occur and, in consequence, the right to strike has not generally led to corresponding legal duties being imposed on others. Italy, however, provides an example of how the right to strike enshrined in the Constitution can lead to specific statutory obligations on others not to interfere with that right. There the right to strike has been reflected in the law relating to unfair dismissal in a provision requiring an employer not to discriminate against or dismiss an employee simply because he has participated in a strike.

362. If, of course, a system of positive rights for Great Britain were to cover other rights (eg the right to associate or to bargain collectively) the problem of corresponding obligations would be enlarged.

(v) Whose rights?

363. If there were to be a positive right to strike (or lock-out) the intention would be for it to be exercised by individual employees (and employers). If there were a right to organise a strike, it would have to apply both to individuals and to trade unions if it were to correspond to the existing legal position.

364. This raises the question of whether there would need to be special treatment of trade unions and employers' associations. As described in paragraphs 104–115, Section 14 of the Trade Union and Labour Relations Act 1974 grants much wider immunity to trade unions and employers' associations than does Section 13 to individuals. If the aim were to leave this position unchanged, this would have to be carried through into a system of positive rights. It is difficult to see how a right corresponding to the existing Section 14 immunity might be formulated since it operates essentially as a means of protecting unions against actions for damages or injunctions for torts (not just those committed in contemplation or furtherance

of a trade dispute). In other words, it is not a means of enabling unions to take positive action but rather, of its nature, a "negative" right. If it were desired to achieve the same position as in existing law, the solution might be to retain something like the present immunity which prevents trade unions and employers' associations from being sued for any wrongful act. This would, of course, mean that the law would consist of a mixture of positive rights and immunities.

Enforcement

365. A system of positive rights has, in most countries, been accompanied by its own procedures for enforcement. This has meant devising sanctions for those who infringe or overstep the right to strike and deciding which courts are to administer and enforce those sanctions.

366. The nature of sanctions depends to a large extent on how the positive rights are defined and limited. For example, if, as in Italy, the right to strike were supported by a corresponding duty on an employer not to dismiss an employee for going on strike, then the remedy for an aggrieved employee might more naturally be an application to an industrial tribunal as in other cases of unfair dismissal.

367. The main consideration, however, is the sanction to be applied to those who overstep the right to strike by taking unlawful industrial action. There are three main questions which would need to be resolved.

368. First, what is to be the nature of the wrong? At present, those who are not protected by the legal immunities are liable at common law for actions in tort for interfering with contracts. In an alternative system there would need to be some new grounds for legal action to replace the common law remedies. The US legislators of the 1930s and 1940s solved this problem by creating a new offence—the "unfair labor practice". This idea was adopted in this country by the Industrial Relations Act 1971. Under that Act it became possible to bring an action for an unfair industrial practice against the organisers of a strike declared unlawful by the Act; and this remedy was intended to replace the actions in tort available at common law. It is likely that something similar would be needed to complement a legal right to strike (or lock-out).

369. The second question is what remedies should be available to someone who is suffering from unlawful industrial action? In particular, should the main remedies continue to be an injunction and an action for damages? These are the main remedies in most other countries, though in some cases restrictions are placed on the amount of damages which can be awarded. Under the American system the decision whether to seek an injunction against unlawful industrial action rests, not with the employer, but with the General Counsel of the National Labor Relations Board who then takes up the case on behalf of the aggrieved party.

370. Third, which courts are to administer and enforce the law? One option is simply to leave the existing civil courts to administer and enforce

labour law. A feature of several positive rights systems, however, is the labour court, with a separate and distinct jurisdiction. In some systems this is almost completely insulated from the rest of the legal system. In West Germany, for example, there are three tiers of labour courts, with the Federal Labour Court providing the court of final appeal. In other systems the jurisdictions of the labour courts and civil courts overlap. This is particularly marked in the United States, where the National Labor Relations Board hears complaints of unfair industrial practice, with a right of appeal to the Federal Appeal and Supreme Courts. In addition, an employer can of his own accord pursue an action for damages in the district court.

371. It is noteworthy that where positive rights have been introduced by legislation in Great Britain separate labour courts have developed to administer them. Most of the individual employment rights, for example, are in the jurisdiction of the industrial tribunals and the Employment Appeal Tribunal (although appeals from the latter go into the ordinary legal system); some collective rights are enforced through the Central Arbitration Committee.

Positive rights and the common law

372. Another important consideration is the relationship between a positive rights system and the common law. The common law, as has been seen, provides the basic rights and principles which underlie our legal system. It is, therefore, essential that any new system of positive rights takes account of the common law and vice versa. To fail to do so would leave the law in a state of great uncertainty.

373. Difficulties could arise, for example, from the relationship between a positive right to strike and the law of tort. Replacing the existing immunities by an alternative right to strike would, without special provision to the contrary, restore the common law remedies in tort available against the organisers of unlawful industrial action. This would mean that two parallel courses would be open to those damaged by an unlawful strike: either to seek redress through whatever sanctions and penalties were devised for the system of positive rights or to sue in tort for unlawful interference with contract. The existence of statutory and common law rights alongside each other would clearly be a source of confusion. The courts might be expected to decide that a positive right overrode the remedy available at common law; but, of course, if they did not do so the positive right to strike could be nullified by the continuing remedies available in tort.

374. Another area of difficulty, already referred to, would be in relation to the law of contract. Without specific guidance, the courts would have to decide whether a right to strike or lock-out released an individual from his obligations not to break his contract of employment. If it did not do so then, in spite of the right to strike, a person would be liable to be sued for damages if he took industrial action in breach of his contract.

375. Finally, in the absence of specific provision to the contrary, the creation of a positive right to strike could itself give rise to common law

as well as statutory remedies. This is because of the common law maxim "ubi ius, ibi remedium", which expresses the general principle that whenever there exists a "right" recognised at law there exists also a remedy for an infringement of that right, even though no remedy appears to be provided by statute. This could mean, for example, that even if the law were silent on the sanctions available for interference with the right to strike (eg by discriminating against an employee for going on strike), there might nevertheless be a remedy in the civil courts where such interference occurred or where those concerned combined to cause such interference.

376. This suggests that there would be a need to insulate any legal right to strike from the common law and to make it clear that the only remedies available against unlawful industrial action are those enacted by the legislation which establishes the right and not otherwise. This could mean developing a completely separate system of law with its own sanctions and with separate courts to administer and enforce those sanctions. Moreover, the remedies for infringement of the right to strike would presumably have to exclude action taken by the employer in pursuance of his right to lock-out referred to in paragraph 352 above.

Advantages and disadvantages of a positive rights system

377. It is apparent from this analysis that there would be a number of complex legal and technical questions to be resolved in switching from immunities to a system of legal rights. In particular, there could be special difficulty in insulating a right to strike from the common law; a difficulty which could be compounded if some elements of immunity (eg Section 14 of the Trade Union and Labour Relations Act 1974: see paragraph 364 above) had to co-exist with positive rights. To a certain extent, the success of a positive rights system would depend on how successfully these problems could be overcome.

378. In considering the merits of a positive rights system it can be misleading to suppose that the provision of a positive right to strike would necessarily impose further restrictions on union power. Many who favour such restrictions are attracted by a legal system based on positive rights. There is, however, nothing in a positive rights system which is inherently more restrictive of trade union power than the present system. As experience of other countries shows, positive rights can accommodate a whole range of different approaches. Whatever legal system is adopted, the policy issues raised in the previous Chapter remain to be settled.

379. The more narrow question considered here is whether a legal system based on positive rights is a more effective way of defining the legal protections and obligations of employees and trade unions than one based on immunities. The advantages which are generally seen in a positive rights system are ones of simplicity and clarity. It is argued that positive rights enable the law to be framed in terms which relate more directly to industrial experience. It is believed that a lot of the misunderstanding about the present law stems from the inherent complexity of the torts concerned and that laymen have difficulty in applying concepts based on the common

law of contract and tort to the reality of industrial disputes. To the extent that a positive rights system succeeded in moving the language and concepts of the law on industrial conflict away from immunities against tortious liability, it might be easier to understand and more straightforward to apply, not just for unions and management but for the courts as well. Indeed, it is possible that a system of positive rights would help remove the unions' traditional suspicion of the courts. The latter have often been seen as anti-union because their function has been to uphold the common law which is based on individual rights. To the extent that a system of positive rights changed that function into one of defending collective rights, the courts might seem more neutral in interpreting the rights of management, unions and workers.

380. It is a matter of judgement how far these benefits could be achieved. But three points seem to emerge from the examination of a positive rights system undertaken in this Chapter. First, though the language of positive rights can be more easily related to industrial reality, this does not necessarily make for a simpler legislative provision. There appears to be no escape from a detailed provision which carefully defines and constrains the application of a right to strike. Secondly, however carefully defined, there would always remain under this and under any other system some uncertainty at the margin about whether a particular action was lawful or not. Thirdly, there is no indication that a positive rights system would be any less open to judicial interpretation than a system of immunities. There would always be difficult cases for the courts to decide. Indeed, an entirely new legal framework would be likely to open up new areas of uncertainty until a corpus of judicial interpretation had developed.

381. It should be added finally that, of course, the success or failure of a positive rights system would not be judged solely by the clarity of the drafting or the ease of application. It would depend to a large extent on the nature of the rights it established and on the success with which it resolved the conflicting considerations discussed in the previous Chapter.

Conclusion

382. It would undoubtedly be a formidable task to formulate a legal system of positive rights to replace the present law. The whole question would need to be expertly examined. But it would first need to be decided whether there was a positive advantage in the establishment of a new system. The Government would therefore welcome views on the above analysis and, in particular, on the following points:

(i) would it be desirable to make the fundamental change from the present system based on immunities to one based on positive rights?

(ii) would a system of positive rights contribute to an improvement in industrial relations?

(iii) would it be clearer, more easily understood and less complex as a system of law?

(iv) would both employers and unions welcome the obligations that would be involved?

CHAPTER 5

CONCLUSION

383. The Government believe that improvements in our industrial relations are essential to our economic recovery. Our industrial relations have acted as a barrier to increased productivity and efficiency and have been bedevilled by strikes and other forms of industrial action. As a result they have operated in the interests neither of management nor employees and have clearly damaged the interests of the community as a whole. The question is how far improvements in our industrial relations can be brought about by changes in the law. This Green Paper is intended to provide the basis for a full and informed public debate.

384. It is clear from the description of the development of trade union law in Chapter 2 that immunities are not simply legal privileges which could be abolished outright. Without some legal protection—however circumscribed—it would be impossible for trade unions or individuals to organise industrial action without risk of civil proceedings and the ultimate safeguard of a collective withdrawal of labour would be effectively nullified. The debate, therefore, is about the nature and the limits of that legal protection. The experience of other countries where the law provides positive rights rather than immunities suggests that, whatever the nature of this protection, decisions still have to be made about where the limits of lawful industrial action should be drawn.

385. This Green Paper examines two distinct sets of problems. First, it considers a number of propositions which have been made for changes within our existing legal system. Essentially, what is involved in each case is finding a balance between the conflicting needs and interests of those involved: the interests of employers seeking to manage their businesses effectively as against the interests of trade unions in carrying out the function of representing their members; the ability of trade unions to mount effective industrial action as against the need for the individual to be protected against the abuse of trade union power; and the interests of those in dispute and of the rest of the community, including employers and employees who have no connection with the dispute but whose business and jobs may be threatened. Secondly, the Green Paper considers the problems which derive from the complexity and uncertainty of our present contract and tort-based system of law. It is in the interests of everybody that the law in this area should be as clear as possible and be seen to be relevant. The basic question here is whether we should break loose from our present system by replacing it with a system based on positive rights.

386. The Government would welcome the views of industry and others concerned on the issues covered in this Green Paper and the questions raised in Chapters 3 and 4. Comments should be sent before 30 June 1981 to the Department of Employment, Caxton House, Tothill Street, London SW1H 9NF.

APPENDIX

INDUSTRIAL RELATIONS IN OTHER COUNTRIES

1. This Appendix describes industrial relations law in five Western industrial countries: Australia, the Federal Republic of Germany, France, Sweden and the United States of America.

2. It provides a brief, largely factual, account of the main features of the law and practice in each country which are relevant to the issues discussed in this Green Paper. It is not intended to be a comprehensive description of labour law in those countries. That would involve an examination not just of statute law but of how it has been interpreted by the courts. Nor is it an analysis of how the law has worked in practice or how it has affected the development and operation of industrial relations in each country.

3. Some useful comparisons can be drawn between the approach to industrial relations law in Britain and other countries. These are discussed, where they are relevant, in the main text in Chapters 3 and 4. In considering such comparisons, however, it is important to see the experience of other countries against the background of their cultural, social, economic and legal traditions. It is important to remember that, just as the main immunities in Britain have provided the framework of law for over 70 years, many of the main features of other legal systems are equally long established and were introduced at a time when the social and economic conditions were quite different from those today. As the Donovan Commission said when commenting on the fact that, in most other countries, collective agreements are legally enforceable:

> "When dealing with the impact which the law may have on strikes, one must consider the nature of those strikes, and when considering a reform of the law governing collective bargaining and agreements, one must bear in mind the nature of the bargaining process and of the agreements which are its result. This is important if one seeks to draw lessons from the legal experience of other countries. It is sometimes possible to transplant from one country to another legal institutions or principles which have stood the test of time. But to do so may be useless or even harmful if the social conditions of the country which seeks to adopt them differ from those which have given rise to their growth in the country of origin". (paragraph 461).

93

A AUSTRALIA

Employers and unions

4. There are about 2·9 million trade union members representing some 55 per cent of the Australian workforce. There are 315 trade unions, most of them affiliated with State or national bodies. The Australian Council of Trade Unions (ACTU) is the leading national trade union federation in Australia. It comprises both blue and white-collar unions and has an affiliated membership of 2·3 million. Another important federation is the Council of Australian Government Employees' Organisations (CAGEO) which covers unions in the Australian public service and has an affiliated membership of 240,000.

5. There is no single employers' federation. In recent years, to match the great importance of the ACTU, the employers have endeavoured to bring their national bodies closer together. The leading national organisation for employers is the Confederation of Australian Industry.

The legal framework for industrial relations

6. Australia has taken neither the American approach to positive encouragement and regulation of collective bargaining, nor the British approach whereby certain common law rules are excluded by statutory enactment from application to trade unions and their industrial activities. Rather, it has planned alongside the common law statutorily based tribunals to deal with industrial disputes by compulsory conciliation and arbitration.

7. Under the Australian federal system, legal powers are divided between the Commonwealth (Federal) Government and the six States. Federal and State Industrial Tribunals differ in name and style of operation and, in two States, tripartite Wages Boards, rather than fully independent arbitration tribunals, operate. Notification to them by a party to it of the existence of an industrial dispute in each case confers immediate jurisdiction.

8. The basic federal statute is the Conciliation and Arbitration Act 1904. It empowers the Australian Conciliation and Arbitration Commission to settle interstate industrial disputes by conciliation or arbitration. Where conciliation has failed to settle a dispute, the Commission is required to deal with it by arbitration. The Act empowers the Commission to deal with "industrial matters" which include, inter alia, minimum wages, allowances, hours of work and the model terms and conditions of employment. State tribunal awards are similarly enforceable; their jurisdiction is not restricted to interstate disputes.

9. The common law industrial torts of conspiracy to injure, conspiracy to employ illegal means, interference with contractual relationships and intimidation, remain applicable. The general practice, however, is to have recourse to the Commission or to State Industrial Tribunals; the use of common law remedies is very rare. Once the Commission is seized of an industrial dispute, it requires industrial action in support of it to cease.

94

Collective agreements

10. Where the parties to an industrial dispute have reached an agreement, the Commission may certify a memorandum of its terms or make an order giving effect to them. The agreement thereupon becomes enforceable as though it were an award of the Commission. Agreements made between employers and unions in isolation from the arbitration system are enforceable if the union has achieved corporate status by virtue of registration under the 1904 Act, and if the intention to create a binding legal obligation is established.

The right to strike

11. Apart from Commonwealth public servants, strikes are not illegal *per se* by Federal law, but steps may be taken by the aggrieved party, and also by the independent Industrial Relations Bureau, to invoke the penalties available under the Conciliation and Arbitration Act for strikes in breach of an award of the Commission.

12. A strike in furtherance of a secondary boycott may be subject to penalties imposed by the Trade Practices Act, though this is not fully tested.

13. By the law of some States strikes are legally prohibited and subject to penalties; but state law is rarely invoked against strikers or unions.

Trade union liability

14. Every union registered under the Conciliation and Arbitration Act attains corporate status. (Registration confers substantial benefits, including the right for a union to represent its members collectively and to obtain an award through the processes of the Commission). As such, it is corporately liable for any breach of the Act or of the Trade Practices Act, or of an award of the Commission and for any breach of common law duty.

Restrictions on secondary action

15. The Trade Practices Act specifies that it is an offence for a person (including a registered union) in concert with another to engage in a secondary boycott of a corporation the purpose and likely effect of which is to cause substantial damage to that corporation or to lessen competition in any market in which it trades. A union is deemed to be liable for a secondary boycott in which two or more of its members participate unless it shows that it took all reasonable steps to prevent them from participating. Where the Conciliation and Arbitration Commission is notified of such a dispute, an injunction may be stayed and the Commission is empowered to settle the dispute by conciliation.

Picketing

16. There is no Commonwealth legislation specifically directed towards the activity of picketing. But statute law prohibits conduct which in some circumstances could include picketing:

   (a) (i) secondary boycotts by trade unions where the boycotts have both
        the purpose and effect of either substantially damaging a particular
        business or substantially lessening competition in a market;

95

(ii) conduct by trade union members which has the purpose and effect, or likely effect, of preventing or substantially hindering a third person from engaging in interstate or overseas trade or commerce, except where employees are taking action for a dominant purpose substantially related to the remuneration or conditions of employment of themselves or of fellow employees of the same employer: Trade Practices Act.

(b) Threats or intimidation of any kind, boycotts without reasonable call or excuse, whose effect is to obstruct or hinder the transport of goods or passengers in overseas trade, or to prevent the offer or acceptance of employment in such trade: Commonwealth Crimes Act. (This provision is in practice virtually a dead letter).

17. In addition, the Public Order (Protection of Persons and Property) Act makes it an offence unreasonably to obstruct the passage of persons or vehicles into, out of, or on Commonwealth premises, or otherwise in relation to their use. Similar provision is also made in respect of premises used for diplomatic and special missions, consular posts and the residence of their staff. The Act permits a member of any Australian Police Force to arrest persons in certain circumstances for offences against the Act.

18. State legislation covering picketing adopts, either wholly or subject to specific exceptions, the provisions of the English Conspiracy and Protection of Property Act 1875, imposing penal liability for "watching and besetting" a person's house or place of work. Most statute law protects picketing whose purpose is merely to obtain or communicate information. Queensland law protects picketing for the purpose of persuasion, but this must be in contemplation or furtherance of an industrial dispute. English case law is applicable and the effect is that "watching and besetting" is only an offence if it also constitutes a civil tort.

Ballots

19. There is no federal legislation which requires a ballot in relation to strike action. But the Conciliation and Arbitration Commission may, where a federal arbitration award applies, order a secret ballot where it believes that the prevention or ending of industrial action, or a settlement of matters giving rise to it, would be assisted by ascertaining the views of the union's members concerned. Nor does federal legislation require that unions should conduct ballots in relation to changes in their rules, though union rules themselves commonly provide for referenda on proposals for major policy changes.

20. But the Conciliation and Arbitration Act requires that the rules of every registered union must provide that the election of the holder of every office, down to branch level, shall be by secret ballot; where direct voting is provided for it must generally be by secret postal ballot. Unions may choose to have their ballot conducted by the Industrial Registrar's Office or the Australian Electoral Office.

21. Three States—New South Wales, Queensland and Western Australia—also have separate legislation which broadly empowers each State Commission to order a secret ballot of union members in order to establish the support for strike action. The scope and detail of the powers conferred varies in each State. In addition, the Western Australian legislation requires the election of union office holders by secret ballot in the same way as the Commonwealth Conciliation and Arbitration Act.

Essential services

22. Any Commonwealth employee engaged in "industrial action" may be suspended without salary and later dismissed: Commonwealth Employees (Employment Provisions) Act.

23. Any Public Service Officer directly fomenting or taking part in any strike which interferes with the carrying on of any part of the Public Service or utilities is deemed to have committed an illegal act against the peace and good order of Australia and is liable to summary dismissal: Public Service Act.

24. Two States—Queensland and Victoria—have Essential Services Acts which empower the Governor in Council, where it appears that any essential service is likely to be interrupted or dislocated, to proclaim a period of emergency in relation to that service. This allows the appropriate Minister to operate and control the service for a period of up to one month at a time.

Political strikes

25. Political strikes are not the subject of specific federal or State legislation.

Action against non-union labour

26. It is an offence for an employer to dismiss or discriminate against an employee for refusing or failing to join in industrial action, as it is for a union to coerce an employer to take such action.

27. It is an offence for a union to take or threaten to take industrial action against an employer to coerce the employer to take discriminatory action (such as the refusal to supply goods) against a self-employed person or an independent contractor because that person is not a member of an organisation. Such persons are similarly protected from industrial action by unions designed to coerce them to join an organisation.

28. It is, however, the chief object of the Conciliation and Arbitration Act to encourage the organisation of trade unions. The Conciliation and Arbitration Commission is, therefore, able to make awards of qualified or unqualified preference. It cannot, however, make awards of compulsory unionism.

29. The Act empowers the Commission to grant preference of employment to members of registered organisations wherever, in its opinion, it is necessary for:

- the prevention or settlement of an industrial dispute;
- ensuring that effect will be given to the purpose and objectives of an award;
- the maintenance of industrial peace; or
- the welfare of society.

An employer bound by a preference clause is not required to give preference to unionists over persons who hold a conscientious objection certificate. An employer is prohibited from dismissing an employee who holds a conscientious objection certificate or injuring him in his employment or refusing to employ such a person by reason of the fact that he is not a member of an organisation. It is also an offence for an organisation to coerce an employer into taking discriminatory action against such a person.

30. To obtain a conscientious objection certificate, a person must satisfy the Industrial Registrar that his conscientious beliefs do not allow him to be a member of any trade union. "Conscientious beliefs" can be based on religious grounds or any other ground.

31. Preference clauses awarded by the Commission include the following, often in combination:

- preference to unionists in the engagement of employees;
- preference to unionists in a redundancy;
- preference to unionists in the taking of leave;
- preference to unionists in the promotion of staff; and
- preference to unionists in the recruitment of staff where the union has to be informed by the employer of vacancies as they arise and the union is given an opportunity to present members for employment.

Closed shops

32. There is no federal legislation prohibiting closed shop agreements. Protection is, however, afforded to employees with a conscientious objection to membership of any trade union: see paragraph 30, above.

B FEDERAL REPUBLIC OF GERMANY

Employers and unions

33. The Deutscher Gewerkschaftsbund (DGB), the German equivalent of the TUC, was set up in 1949. An early objective was the rationalisation of the pre-war craft unions into a few federated unions each representing a single industry or area of public service. Today, the DGB has 17 such unions and its membership represents about 37 per cent of the workforce. Employers too are organised on an industry basis but into two confederations—the Bundesvereinigung der Deutschen Arbeitgeberverbaende (BDA), which deals with industrial relations and employment matters, and the Bundesverband der Deutschen Industrie (BDI) which deals with the furtherance of wider business interests. Like the unions, both confederations have been set up since the war.

The legal framework for industrial relations

34. West German industrial relations law is based on positive rights guaranteed by the Constitution and by federal law. The basic rights of employers and unions are contained in Article 9 of the Constitution.

35. The law is administered by labour courts (set up in 1926 but substantially revised in 1953). The courts have exclusive jurisdiction in industrial relations and employment matters. Final appeal is to the Federal Labour Court.

36. Within each firm there are statutory works councils and in large companies workers have the right to representation on the supervisory Board.

Legal enforcement of collective agreements

37. Most collective agreements are concluded nationally. Collective agreements are legally enforceable. It is illegal not only to break an agreement, but also to encourage others to do so. Penalties can be applied to individuals or organisations.

Trade union liability

38. German trade unions can sue and be sued like any other organisation except where they take action in line with a collective agreement.

The right to strike

39. There is no formal right to strike as such, but strikes and lockouts are lawful, provided that they are in furtherance of improvements in working and economic conditions and do not break a collective agreement or otherwise break the law. Full time established public servants do not have the right to strike.

Secondary action

40. There is no specific provision in the law to cover secondary action which in any case is rare in West Germany.

Picketing

41. There is no specific provision in German law regarding picketing. It is lawful peacefully to persuade someone to work or not work, so long as it does not break a collective agreement.

Union Ballots

42. There is no legal requirement to hold a ballot before calling a strike. However, all but one of the DGB unions are bound by their own rules not to call industrial action unless approved by 75 per cent of those concerned in a secret ballot.

Essential services

43. There are no statutory limitations on strikes in essential services. But the DGB keeps a close central control over planned action in certain sectors. A union planning a strike in an essential service has to notify the DGB beforehand and provide details of emergency measures necessary to maintain essential services.

Political strikes

44. Political strikes are illegal under the Constitution, which allows only industrial action which is aimed at improving working and economic conditions.

Coercion of non-union labour

45. The Constitution guarantees the freedom to join or not to join a union, which has the effect of making unlawful all coercion to join a union.

Closed shop

46. For the same reason the closed shop is illegal in West Germany.

C FRANCE

Employers and unions

47. Little more than 20 per cent of all French workers are trade union members. Membership is highest in the public sector and in major manufacturing firms. In most private companies membership rarely exceeds 10 per cent. The French trade union movement is divided on religious and political lines. Three main rival confederations compete for members from all sectors. In contrast, employers are highly organised. About 90 per cent of firms are members of the Conseil National du Patronat Français (CNPF) (roughly equivalent to the CBI) and adhere closely to its policies. Many of the rest belong to the Confédération des Petites et Moyennes Entreprises (CPME)—representing medium and small sized firms.

The legal framework for industrial relations

48. French industrial relations law is based on "positive rights" guaranteed to individuals in the Constitution and the Labour Code (which codifies all labour legislation and relevant court decisions). These rights include the right to strike, the right to negotiate, the right to be represented by and organised in a trade union and also the freedom to work and not to join a trade union.

49. Collective rights have traditionally been merely the sum of the individual rights of the group concerned.

50. Collective disputes are dealt with through the normal legal system, as are appeals from the "conseils de prud' hommes" (roughly equivalent to British industrial tribunals) which deal with disputes about individual rights. There is scope for conciliation and arbitration outside the legal system.

Legal enforcement of collective agreements

51. Most collective agreements are concluded nationally, usually on an industry basis. Every collective agreement is legally enforceable as a civil contract. Such agreements are binding on all employees covered—whether union members or not. It is not uncommon for employers and unions to accuse one another of failure to observe the terms of collective agreements, but the actual extent of non-compliance is difficult to determine.

52. Individual contracts between employers and employees are also binding.

Trade union liability

53. Some uncertainty has arisen recently about the extent of trade union liability for the actions of their members. Traditionally, French law has considered the individual, not his union, responsible for the consequences of industrial action. Hence unions have no specific rights, obligations or

immunities in connection with industrial action. However, there has been an increase in recent years in the number of civil actions brought against trade unions involved in disputes and some (but not all) of these actions have been successful.

The right to strike

54. The French Constitution guarantees the individual worker the right to strike. Under Article L.521-1 of the Labour Code "a strike does not break the employment contract in the absence of a serious fault ('faute lourde') on the part of the employee". However, the courts have interpreted this concept in ways which restrict the scope for industrial action. The following are unlawful:

- "Illicit" action involving, for example, breach of a collective agreement or working to rule, restricting output, or rotating strikes where one group after another stop work for a short period;

- Any action which damages the employer's property.

Other restrictions on the right to strike are described in paragraphs 58 and 59.

Restrictions on secondary action

55. Secondary action in furtherance of a dispute is rare in France and there is no specific provision covering such action in French law.

Picketing

56. It is not an offence in French law to seek peacefully to persuade someone to work or not to work but it is a criminal offence to *impede* him in the exercise of his right to work, so that intimidatory picketing is illegal. Occupation of the premises involved in a dispute is more common than picketing although this too is illegal.

Trade union ballots

57. There are no legal provisions requiring ballots to be taken before strikes are called and this rarely happens in practice. However, the rules of trade unions, which are confirmed by Ministerial decree, all contain provision for ballots for the election of officials. At national level this may take the form of a card vote at the biennial or triennial conference. French unions do not conduct postal ballots.

Essential services

58. The right to strike is limited for certain groups of workers as follows:

(i) certain public servants may not strike. They include the armed forces, police and air traffic controllers;

(ii) striking radio and television workers are required to maintain a minimum service;

102

(iii) teachers are required to ensure that children are kept on school premises under school supervision during normal teaching hours when the schools are on strike;

(iv) workers in nuclear power stations may not take industrial action which imperils safety.

It should be noted, however, that, despite the legal prohibitions, there have been strikes of, for example, air-traffic controllers and that on occasion teachers do not respect the obligation referred to in sub-paragraph (iii) above.

Political strikes

59. Lawful industrial action is limited to that which is intended to promote the strikers' *employment* interests ("les intérêts professionels") as opposed to their interests as *citizens*. In theory, therefore, a political strike is not lawful. Some court judgements have interpreted "les intérêts professionels" widely and in 1971 a general strike in defence of jobs, wages and trade union rights was held to be lawful.

Coercion of non-union labour

60. The coercion of non-union members is not generally seen as a problem in France. French workers have a fundamental right not to join a union which makes unlawful all coercion to join a union.

Closed shop

61. The closed shop is illegal in France but in a few sectors, notably the Paris press and the docks where there is a high level of union membership, "de facto" closed shops operate.

D SWEDEN

Employers and unions

62. About 90 per cent of manual and 70 per cent of non-manual workers are trade union members. Membership of employer organisations is similarly high. There are three central union confederations: one (the largest) representing manual workers and the others representing white collar and professional unions respectively. The Swedish employers confederation exercises strong central control over its members.

The legal framework for industrial relations

63. Swedish industrial relations law is based on "positive rights" guaranteed to individuals and collective bodies in the Constitution and in legislation. These rights include the right to strike, the right to negotiate and the right to be represented by, and organised in, a trade union.

64. Swedish labour law is administered through a Labour Court composed of representatives of the judiciary and of employers and unions. The decisions of the Court are final.

The right to strike

65. The Constitution states:

"Any trade union and any employer or association of employers shall have the right to take strike or lock-out actions or any similar measures, except as otherwise provided by law or ensuing from a contract".

The most important exception, and therefore limitation to this right, is the "peace obligation" during the period of validity of a collective agreement. In addition, the Act on the Joint Regulation of Working Life sets out a number of circumstances in which a stoppage of work, blockade, boycott or other action of a similar nature is unlawful: viz where action is taken in order to:

(a) exert pressure in a dispute about an existing collective agreement or about the terms of the Act;

(b) change an existing agreement;

(c) enforce a provision which is to come into force on the expiry of the agreement;

(d) assist others who may not themselves take industrial action.

Collective agreements

66. Bargaining in Sweden is highly centralised. Collective agreements are generally concluded at national level, usually covering a wide range of matters and running for a fixed period of between one and three years.

67. Collective agreements are enforceable at law under the Act on the Joint Regulation of Working Life. In some cases, the confederations have issued "joint recommendations" which are not binding on their affiliates. However, the courts have ruled that non-enforceable agreements are invalid.

Trade union liability

68. Trade union funds are at risk for unlawful action by trade union officials, but not for unlawful action by trade union members unless it is taken on union instructions.

Restrictions on secondary action

69. There are no legislative provisions covering secondary action which is uncommon in Sweden. Any act which contravened a collective agreement would, of course, be unlawful.

Picketing

70. Picketing is relatively uncommon in Sweden. It is lawful peacefully to persuade someone to work or not to work, but it is unlawful actually to prevent someone working who wanted to. It would, of course, be unlawful to break a collective agreement.

Ballots

71. There is no legal requirement for trade union ballots, but the rules of some trade unions do require ballots to be held.

Essential services

72. There are a few restrictions on industrial action in the public sector, though not in the public utilities. Employees in this sector may take part in industrial action only if a trade union initiates it. Most industrial action for political ends is banned.

Political strikes

73. A political strike is not in principle unlawful except for public sector workers (see paragraph 72 above).

Action against non-union labour

74. Because of the historically high level of trade union organisation there is often intense social pressure to join a union in Sweden and most employees do so as a normal part of their employment. It would be unlawful to take industrial action against non-union members while a collective agreement was in force.

Closed shops

75. The closed shop is not illegal, but it is estimated that not more than 5 per cent of Swedish workers are covered by closed shop agreements. These are in the building, printing and transport industries. Because of the high degree of unionisation the closed shop is not a controversial issue. Nonetheless, the Swedish employers' association forbids its members to make closed shop agreements.

E THE UNITED STATES OF AMERICA

Employers and unions

76. Only 22 per cent of American workers are trade union members (compared with 35 per cent in 1945). Unions remain strong in some traditional areas—engineering, cars, mines, steelworks, railways—and are actually expanding in the public services. The central confederation (AFL-CIO) is influential but several major unions are not affiliated. There are three main employer confederations all of which act as a strong force against the further development of trade union organisation.

The legal framework for industrial relations

77. US labour legislation is based on positive rights guaranteed by the Constitution, federal law, and state law, and accompanied by a system of immunities to remove impediments to trade union activity under the common law.

78. The basic code of US labour legislation is the Labor Management Relations Act 1947 (the Taft Hartley Act). This provides the legal framework for the conduct of industrial relations and contains the restrictions on industrial action which are described in the rest of this Appendix. The Act is administered by the National Labor Relations Board (NLRB) which acts as an industrial court, hearing complaints of unfair industrial practice brought under the Act.

Collective agreements

79. Collective agreements in the US are legally enforceable. Most agreements contain elaborate grievance procedures and "no-strike clauses", or clauses which allow strikes only in certain defined circumstances.

The right to strike

80. The courts have ruled that neither the Constitution nor the common law provides an absolute right to strike. The federal law imposes considerable restrictions on the right to strike. The following are unlawful:

(a) strikes during the period of a collective agreement where, as is usual, the contract contains a no-strike clause or a grievance procedure and arbitration clause;

(b) strikes for purposes which constitute an "unfair labor practice" under the Taft Hartley Act;

(c) strikes which employ unlawful means;

(d) strikes where the dispute is not between employer and employee;

(e) strikes of public servants working for the Federal or State governments. (There are exceptions in a few states where such strikes are permitted).

Trade union liability

81. Unions are liable for damages if their members take unlawful industrial action. In practice, however, the courts do not usually hold the trade union responsible if it has clearly and specifically withheld its authority.

Restrictions on secondary action

82. The law in this area is complex and there has been considerable litigation on the question of what constitutes secondary action.

83. Basically, industrial action is lawful if it is taken against a party to the dispute, but not otherwise. As a result, almost all secondary action (ie activity directed against a third party or so-called "neutral") is actionable as an "unfair labor practice". The main exception is activity against an employer who has lost his neutrality by performing work for the employer involved in a labour dispute which, but for the strike, would have been done by that employer himself. In such an instance, the employer taking on the work is viewed as an "ally" of the employer who is the object of the strike and is therefore held to have become a party to the dispute.

Picketing

84. The law on picketing is complex and the subject of a large amount of case law.

85. As a consequence of the constitutional right of freedom of speech, the law protects "informational picketing", as long as it does not seek to stop anyone from working. This basic right has been limited by the federal law, both through specific restrictions on picketing and through general "unfair labor practice" provisions. Picketing is unlawful, for example, where it involves:

(a) obstructing entry to an employer's premises (the courts usually grant an injunction restricting pickets to two per entrance);

(b) picketing premises of an employer not in dispute (unless the employer has done something to help the employer in dispute—this applies in most cases);

(c) picketing in a recognition dispute when picketing continues for more than 30 days and the union seeking recognition has not applied for a secret ballot to be conducted by the government or where for one of several reasons (eg employees are currently represented by another union) recognition cannot be extended lawfully; and

(d) interfering with employees of another employer at a site where there is more than one employer. (Often employers working on common sites establish so-called "reserve gates" that are to be used exclusively by employees of neutral employers. Picketing at such gates on a common site is unlawful).

Picketing which involves "serious misconduct", such as violence or threatening behaviour, constitutes an "unfair labor practice".

Ballots

86. There is no federal law requiring ballots before a strike (except in the case of strikes in essential industries—see paragraph 87 below). However, several States make specific provision for this and many unions hold ballots voluntarily. Federal law also requires the use of secret ballots in local union elections and in electing delegates to union bodies at national and intermediate level. The law also states that the election of officers must take place at least every five years at national level, at least every four years at intermediate level and at least every three years at local level.

Essential Services

87. Under the Taft Hartley Act,[1] if the President thinks a strike will affect a whole industry or "imperil the national health and safety" he may appoint a "board of inquiry" to investigate and report on the facts of the dispute. He may then ask the Attorney-General to seek an injunction to restrain the strike and appoint another board of enquiry to advise him on the dispute. There then follows a cooling off period of 80 days, towards the end of which the NLRB must hold a secret ballot of employees concerned on the employer's last offer. If the employees reject the offer the injunction is lifted and the strike may go ahead. But the President has then to submit a report to Congress with recommendations for further action.

Political strikes

88. Under federal law a strike may be protected, unprotected or unlawful depending on the circumstances. For example, employees who strike over their employer's "unfair labor practices" generally receive the full protection of the federal law—their employment may not be terminated and they are entitled to reinstatement to their jobs at the end of the dispute. On the other hand, employees who engage in an unprotected strike (eg a strike in breach of a contract agreement not to strike) forfeit a large part of the law's protection, while employees who engage in an unlawful strike (eg a strike for an unlawful object such as a particular work assignment) lose the protection of federal law entirely. Political strikes—which are extremely rare—are not protected by law. In the United States, strikes generally involve only employees of the employer in dispute and arise either over their terms and conditions of employment or because they believe that their employer has engaged in "unfair labor practices".

Action against non-union labour

89. The Taft Hartley Act guarantees the rights of employees not to be union members.

---

[1] The Taft Hartley Act bans strikes in the federal service. Laws governing the State employee vary considerably, although every State prohibits strikes by police and fire service employees.

Closed Shops

90. Despite providing a right not to belong to a union, the Taft Hartley Act allows for "union shops" (post-entry closed shops). However, US law does not allow an employee to be dismissed from a job covered by a union shop agreement except on the grounds that he has failed to pay his dues.

91. The Federal law can be overriden by State law on the closed shop. As a result the closed shop is unlawful in the twenty "right to work" states —mainly in the South. In many cases, unions have sought to get round this via "agency shops" (where employees have to pay union dues but are not bound by the unions rules).

LIST OF STATUTES

LIST OF CASES

LIST OF DOCUMENTS

"Royal Commission on Trade Unions and Employers' Associations (1965–8) Report": Chairman: Lord Donovan (June 1968, Cmnd 3623, HMSO).

"In Place of Strife. A Policy for Industrial Relations". (January 1969, Cmnd 3888, HMSO).

"Report of Inquiry into certain Trade Union Recruitment Activities": conducted by Mr Andrew Leggatt QC (October 1980, Cmnd 7706, HMSO).

"Code of Practice on Closed Shop Agreements and Arrangements". Department of Employment (November 1980, HMSO).

www.ingramcontent.com/pod-product-compliance
Lightning Source LLC
Chambersburg PA
CBHW030539270326
41927CB00008B/1443